# Environmental Diplomacy

# Environmental Diplomacy

*Negotiating More Effective Global Agreements*

**Lawrence E. Susskind**
*M.I.T.—Harvard Public Disputes Program*

New York   Oxford
OXFORD UNIVERSITY PRESS
1994

Oxford University Press

Oxford New York Toronto
Delhi Bombay Calcutta Madras Karachi
Kuala Lumpur Singapore Hong Kong Tokyo
Nairobi Dar es Salaam Cape Town
Melbourne Auckland Madrid

and associated companies in
Berlin Ibadan

Library of Congress Cataloging-in-Publication Data
Susskind, Lawrence.
Environmental diplomacy:
negotiating more effective global agreements /
Lawrence E. Susskind.
p.   cm.   Includes index.
ISBN 0-19-507593-5.
—ISBN 0-19-507594-3 (pbk.)
1. Environmental law, International.
2. Sustainable development—Law and legislation.
I. Title.
K3585.4.S87   1993   341.7′62—dc20   93-14891

9 8 7 6 5 4 3 2 1

Printed in the United States of America
on acid-free, recycled paper

*For Leslie, who understands*

# Preface

I am not an environmentalist—not if that means advocating protection of natural resources at any cost. Nor am I blindly prodevelopment. Clearly, we've got to feed, clothe, shelter, and find productive work for billions of people, but we ought to be able to accomplish these goals in a way that leaves future generations at least as well off as we are.

As the world's population grows, our task becomes increasingly difficult. Many nations do not have adequate resources to meet even the most basic needs of their citizens, let alone the resources they will need to feed millions of additional mouths in the future. In the meantime, some of the wealthier nations have taken their resource endowments for granted—wasting energy, allowing land to become unproductive, polluting water supplies, and poisoning the air—all in the name of economic growth.

Environmental activists and advocates of sustainable development have pressed for changes in domestic policies in both developing and developed nations. In Europe, the United States, and several other places, substantial progress has been made: conservation efforts are under way and pollution levels have stopped climbing. Indeed, in some of these countries most resource management decisions are now made with much greater attention to minimizing environmental impacts and achieving sustainability. In a good portion of the developing world there is grudging acceptance that economic growth and wise resource management need not be traded off against each other; and the rapid rise of nongovernmental groups devoted to this proposition, even in some of the poorest nations of the world, suggests that the prospects for the future are improving.

However, just as environmental progress is about to be achieved at the domestic level, at least in some parts of the world, the environmental agenda is shifting. Now the most pressing environmental problems are global, including ozone depletion, pollution of the oceans, loss of biodiversity, and potentially devastating climate changes. The resources that need protecting are common resources—fisheries, endangered species, rivers, oceans, forests, and the like that transcend national boundaries. Countries that have learned how to make environmental regulations and control development will, unfortunately, not be able to solve these global problems on their own. And countries still struggling with the burdens of poverty, famine, and war do not see themselves in a position to help.

How will we achieve the level of global cooperation needed to tackle this new generation of environmental threats? We don't have much to work with—only the United Nations (which has not had much success) and a handful of multilateral organizations. Although there are a great many individuals and nongovernmental groups throughout the world eager to assist, coordinating a global response, sometimes in the face of active resistance, is extremely difficult.

In June 1992 the world's attention was focused briefly on these global environmental problems, when ten of thousands of official delegates and unofficial activists met in Brazil at an "Earth Summit" sponsored by the United Nations. After two years of elaborate preparatory meetings, 178 countries attempted to negotiate a series of international environmental treaties. Conference organizers managed to get more heads of state to the conference than had ever gathered before, but they were not able to complete even a small portion of the agenda assigned to them by the General Assembly of the United Nations. This worries me, and I think it should worry you as well.

We must find other ways of ensuring the level of collective action required to address the next generation of global environmental threats. To do this, the art and science of environmental diplomacy must be enhanced. Diplomats, politicians, environmental action groups, scientists, business leaders, journalists, and many others will need to find new ways of working together. We will have to weave together knowledge and skills from the fields of international relations, environmental science, negotiation, law, economics, and other fields to build the necessary institutional capacity. It will not help, the way it sometimes does, to break the problem into smaller, more manageable, pieces. Only a comprehensive global approach to managing environmental resources and coordinating sustainable development will work.

*Wilmot Flat, N.H.*                                                                              L.E.S.
*March 1993*

# Contents

# Abbreviations

| | |
|---|---|
| ATS | Antarctic Treaty System |
| CITES | Convention on International Trade in Endangered Species of Wild Flora and Fauna |
| CMS | Conservation of Migratory Species of Wild Animals |
| CFC | chlorofluorocarbon |
| CCAMLR | Convention on the Conservation of Antarctic Marine Living Resources |
| CRAMRA | Convention on the Regulation of Antarctic Mineral Resources Activities |
| EC | European Community |
| EC Commission | Commission of the European Communities |
| ECOSOC | UN Economic and Social Council |
| ECE | UN Economic Commission for Europe |
| EMEP | Cooperative Program for Monitoring and Evaluation of the Long-Range Transmission of Air Pollution in Europe |
| EPA | U.S. Environmental Protection Agency |
| GAI | "Green" Amnesty International |
| GATT | General Agreement on Tariffs and Trade |
| GEF | Global Environmental Facility |
| GEMS | Global Environmental Monitoring System |
| HCFC | hydrochlorofluorocarbon |
| IAEA | International Atomic Energy Agency |
| ICEL | International Council on Environmental Law |
| ICSU | International Council of Scientific Unions |
| IENN | International Environmental Negotiation Network |
| IMO | International Maritime Organization |
| IPCC | Intergovernmental Panel on Climate Change |
| IUCN | International Union for the Conservation of Nature (now called World Conservation Union) |
| IWC | International Whaling Commission |
| IWRB | International Waterfowl and Wetlands Research Bureau |

| | |
|---|---|
| LDC | London Dumping Convention |
| MARPOL | International Convention for the Prevention of Pollution from Ships |
| NAFTA | North American Free Trade Agreement |
| NGI | nongovernmental interest group |
| NGO | nongovernmental organization |
| NIEO | New International Economic Order |
| ODA | official development aid |
| OECD | Organization of Economic Cooperation and Development |
| RAMSAR | Convention on Wetlands of Importance Especially as Waterfowl Habitat |
| TFAP | Tropical Forestry Action Plan |
| UN | United Nations |
| UNCED | UN Conference on Environment and Development |
| UNCLOS | UN Convention on the Law of the Sea |
| UNDP | UN Development Programme |
| UNEP | UN Environment Programme |
| UNESCO | UN Educational, Scientific, and Cultural Organization |
| UNITAR | UN Institute for Training and Research |
| WWF | World Wildlife Federation |

# Environmental Diplomacy

# CHAPTER 1

# What Is This Book About?

Suppose you were asked to serve on your nation's delegation to an international conference charged with negotiating a global environmental treaty. There is an ever-increasing number of such negotiations on topics ranging from ozone depletion to ocean pollution, from preserving tropical forests to global warming. And, there are literally billions of stakeholders, including representatives of business and industry, environmental activist groups, and scientific organizations, all of whom insist on being consulted, if not actually included, in such negotiations. Hence, being invited to serve on such a delegation is not an outlandish premise. What problems would you face and how would you handle them?

To participate, you would have to digest a great many technical and scientific reports. Much of this material, you would find, is speculative; that is, it talks about what might happen but acknowledges that much is uncertain. Our collective wisdom about global environmental ecosystems and how they are likely to react to various human interventions is still quite skimpy. Nevertheless, because the risks associated with severe damage to the biosphere are so frightening, your delegation (as well as the teams from other countries) has no choice but to take some kind of action at the international conference.

You would quickly find yourself facing pressure from numerous interest groups, each eager to influence your thinking about how to define the risks and what ought to be done about them. Some groups will not be represented directly on the negotiating committee, so they will have no choice but to rely on you and other delegates to express their concerns. In addition, your delegation will face strong external demands from other national delegations with different needs and priorities. Longtime allies may turn out to be adversaries on certain environmental matters.

The greater the number of countries involved, the more difficult it will be to generate global agreement, yet that is what is required. Global environmental threats are of growing concern to a broad cross-section of groups within each country as well as to a growing number of countries. Transboundary environmental problems like climate change, the preservation of biodiversity, protection of the oceans, decisions about how best to manage shared resources like Antarctica, or the difficult task of promoting sustainable development go well beyond anything one country or even a group of countries can accomplish on its own.

Ultimately, your negotiating committee will be expected to advocate your country's national interests and to speak with a single voice. Yet, the more diverse the membership of your committee, the more difficult it will be to achieve internal consensus. It was disconcerting, for example, to the president of the United States to learn that members of the U.S. Negotiating Committee at the 1992 "Earth Summit" in Brazil disagreed publicly with his stated position on the Biodiversity Convention (which he refused to sign). If your own team is pulling in different directions, it is all but impossible to be effective in a multilateral negotiation.

Negotiating committees usually receive explicit instructions from the most senior levels of their governments, including—in the case of the United States—the White House, the State Department, and a variety of federal agencies, including the Environmental Protection Agency. Indeed, it is not unusual to have technical specialists from these agencies assigned to work with a negotiating committee or even to be members of it.

Unfortunately, individual federal agencies frequently have different priorities and agendas. The State Department, for example, will not want the negotiating committee to take a position on an environmental issue that might damage ongoing relationships with allies, or undermine bilateral discussions concerning collective security or economic aid. The Environmental Protection Agency will want to be certain that all positions taken by the negotiating committee are consistent with prevailing environmental laws and regulations within the United States, so that its domestic enforcement efforts will not be undercut. Key congressional representatives will want to be heard, and some may even demand to be included on the negotiating committee (in part, to be certain that the views of the party out of power are not ignored). Many of these representatives will be primarily interested in promoting regional concerns. For example, they could well oppose a treaty that might hurt their section of the country, even if it helped the rest of the country or, indeed, the rest of the world.

In addition to a whirlpool of conflicting pressures from various governmental representatives, the negotiating committee will also face demands from two other sources, neither of which speaks with anything approaching a single voice: grass-roots environmental groups and such private-sector interests as transportation, energy, and agriculture. Some corporate leaders, concerned that new regulations might increase operating costs, inhibit expansion, or undermine the value of their investments, will launch major lobbying efforts in opposition.

The nongovernmental grass-roots groups, though they rarely speak with one voice, remain a potent political force. Environmental groups range from out-and-out conservationists who oppose any further development in sensitive areas to "free marketeers" who believe that only pricing strategies and financial incentives, not regulations, will be effective in achieving greater environmental protection. Other nongovernmental interests, whether represented on the negotiating committee or not, will work to push the committee in still other directions: consumer advocates will fight to ensure that environmental regulations do not increase the burdens on the poor and the disadvantaged; real estate developers worry that local investment options could be limited by new environmental restrictions contained in international treaties; bankers are wary of the impact that new environmental regulations might have on economic growth; and spokespeople for various scientific groups want to ensure that all policy decisions take account of the "best" technical research available—especially the work that they have done.

Assuming that a negotiating committee can reconcile all these competing internal interests (which is no easy task), it then must deal with the demands of delegations from more than 175 countries—each with its own delicately balanced political agenda, each also dealing with the same kind of multifaceted internal pressures your delegation faces. Included among these countries are democracies as well as dictatorships; nations struggling with the incredible burdens of poverty, famine, and rapid population growth as well as those with substantial gross national products per capita; newly industrializing or reindustrializing countries with little, if any, environmental enforcement; and highly developed countries with elaborate environmental management systems.

This book explores how best to structure global environmental negotiations so that the internal and external pressures on national negotiating committees can be addressed effectively. Obviously, such negotiations must take account of each country's desire (and right!) to pursue its national interests while recognizing the absolute necessity of promoting effective cooperation if we are going to preserve and protect the biosphere. This, then, is why global environmental negotiations are so difficult. We must find a way to do better.

Consider, for example, the much-ballyhooed Earth Summit in Rio de Janeiro. Preparations for this mega-event, attended by 4,000 official and 30,000 unofficial negotiators, took many years. It culminated in a mere two weeks of face-to-face interaction, during which the negotiators tried to work out the details of several incredibly complex agreements. In the fall of 1989, when the United Nations General Assembly called for the Conference on Environment and Development (as it was officially titled), there was some hope that treaties dealing with climate change, transboundary air pollution, deforestation, soil loss, desert expansion and drought, conservation of biological diversity, protection of the oceans and seas, protection of freshwater resources, and strategies for financing all these improvements could be signed in Rio.

In the end, the conferees managed to sign only two treaties: a convention on climate change and a convention on biological diversity. These documents must still be ratified by at least 60 of the legislative branches of the 150-plus governments that signed. The leaders present in Rio also initialed a general declaration of concern about the environment, called the Rio Declaration, supported a long list of "action projects" called Agenda 21, and drafted statements of principles to guide future treaty making on forest protection and desert expansion. They were unable, however, to muster a commitment for even a small portion of the estimated $125 billion in annual contributions needed to implement such a package.

The fact that the Rio de Janeiro delegates succeeded in reaching any agreement at all is a testament to growing worldwide concern about the environmental threats facing the planet. Leaders from all parts of the world were under tremendous pressure to show progress of some sort. Yet, the two treaties that did emerge are, for the most part, only very general statements of concern, or what are called "framework conventions." The Climate Change Convention includes neither timetables nor targets for reducing the emission of the so-called greenhouse gases that are blamed for global warming trends. The Biodiversity Convention was unacceptable to the United States, which charged that it did not adequately protect intellectual property rights and would discourage technological innovation.

The task of generating international agreement on *anything* is extremely difficult. And environmental issues, which combine scientific uncertainty with politics, citizen and industry activism with economics, are probably the most complicated and difficult of all to resolve. Unfortunately, the procedures we currently use to formulate global agreements were not designed to handle the unique demands of environmental problem solving. Moreover, they fail to take account of what we have learned about the dynamics of multi-issue, multiparty negotiation. These procedures accept as given the structure of the United Nations and its sister institutions, even though these organizations were not designed to handle global resource management questions. Indeed, they have been relatively ineffective in promoting the kind of worldwide collaboration required to handle these problems.

Too few people realize that the processes we use to negotiate global agreements are as important as the technical capabilities and the scientific understanding that the negotiators bring to the bargaining table. In fact, good technical solutions are often unattainable because the negotiators are not able to overcome the cultural, ideological, and political differences that divide them. A new consensus-building process is required, and the institutional arrangements on which we have relied must be changed. We also need to rebuild productive working relationships between the developed nations of the North and the developing nations of the South, which have deteriorated markedly in recent years. The current schism between the North and the South makes progress on environmental issues almost impossible.

Based on a close look at fifteen major environmental treaty-making efforts, including those culminating at the Rio Earth Summit, I have identified four procedural shortcomings that account for most of the failures of global environmental negotiation:

- representation and voting procedures do not guarantee that all countries and interests are treated fairly;
- scientific and political considerations are not balanced in ways that ensure that the wisest possible agreements will emerge;
- linkages among environmental concerns and other policy issues are rarely explored or crafted adequately; and
- effective monitoring and enforcement arrangements are not implemented.

These shortcomings are evident to some extent in other kinds of multilateral negotiations, especially those involving international security and trade. They are more pronounced, however, in global environmental treaty negotiations and must be handled differently. While there are surely things to learn from these other types of treaty negotiations, the differences are not insignificant. The importance of scientific considerations, the need to involve large numbers of nongovernmental groups, and the overwhelming uncertainty surrounding both the scope and dynamics of ecological change, require a unique approach to environmental diplomacy. Thus, I have focused almost exclusively on the ways in which these shortcoming present themselves in the environmental treaty-making arena.

Until ways of overcoming these shortcomings are found, global environmental negotiations are not likely to produce adequate results, regardless of how well prepared the individual negotiators are. Although additional global treaties may be signed, they are not likely to accomplish their intended objectives. And, in some instances, years of debate may well end with no agreement at all.

This book provides what I hope will be viewed as a framework for understanding the current way we negotiate global environmental treaties and a guide that offers practical advice on how we can do better. I have concentrated on global, not regional agreements. Regional negotiations among large numbers of countries, especially sets of countries facing markedly different ecological, economic, and cultural circumstances provide important clues as to how we might handle global environmental treaty negotiations more effectively. Bilateral treaty negotiations, however, or those involving small clusters of countries facing mostly similar conditions are less relevant even though they concern the management of natural resources or responses to environmental threats of various kinds.

In Chapter 2, I describe the steps typically involved in formulating conventions and protocols, the two types of global environmental agreements that nations have signed in recent years. I review the inadequacies of high-sounding statements that fail to mandate specific action. I also point out the weaknesses of regulations that are drawn too narrowly to do any good. I explain why most environmental treaty-drafting efforts have fallen victim to the demand that national sovereignty not be abridged, the inherent weaknesses of our international legal system, and the mishandling of scientific uncertainty. In addition, I examine the growing hostility between North and South that threatens to derail most global treaty-making efforts.

In Chapter 3, I look more closely at the first procedural problem— representation and voting—and consider why countries are or are not inclined to participate in global environmental negotiations and the sources of bargaining power that each can tap. Relatively few countries have signed all the global environmental treaties ratified over the past twenty years; many have signed only a few. It is my contention that this is because a few powerful nations play an unnecessarily dominant role in most treaty negotiations, forcing other countries and nongovernmental interests to accept secondary roles or to sit on the sidelines.

Chapter 4, focuses on the dangers of "advocacy science": the misuse of technical information by countries seeking to advance their short-term national interests. I also look at the prospects for formulating "self-correcting" treaties that can incorporate new scientific knowledge about environmental impacts and global change as it emerges.

Chapter 5 delves into the concept of linkage. In my view, unless the participants in global environmental treaty-making negotiations broaden their scope to encompass population growth and the need for more sustainable patterns of development, unconstrained development trends will negate any environmental improvements that future treaties might achieve. Furthermore, unless we find ways of encouraging wealthier countries to help struggling nations meet tougher environmental standards, there will be no hope of bridging the growing chasm between North and South.

Chapter 6 deals with the difficulties of ensuring compliance with global environmental treaties, especially in the face of continued demands that national sovereignty not be compromised. I do not believe it is necessary to trade sovereignty to achieve compliance. I believe we can move toward nearly self-enforcing agreements that ensure compliance while guaranteeing sovereignty. The key is to encourage individual nations and groups of countries to make continuous adjustments in their policies and programs in light of what is learned about the true benefits and costs of environmental protection.

Finally, in Chapter 7, I try to pull together a range of recommendations aimed at overcoming the weaknesses of our environmental treaty-making institutions. These reforms do not require radical transformation of existing multilateral arrangements, nor do they depend on changes in leadership in countries that have been reluctant thus far to take part in global environmental negotiations.

I am especially enthusiastic about a new system of *sequenced negotiation* that will move us away from the convention-protocol approach and toward a multistep process that synchronizes worldwide expectations and moves systematically—following a prescribed schedule—from Level I treaties (that spell out principles, definitions, timetables, contingent targets, and responsibilities) to Level II treaties (that require commitments to minimal levels of performance in exchange for explicit sets of benefits), then to Level III treaties (that offer maximum benefits for maximum effort and are based on what can be learned from shared efforts to monitor performance and compliance).

The analyses and proposals presented in this book have evolved over the past several years through continuous interactions with a great many scholars, diplomats, activists, and negotiation practitioners. In late 1989 the Dana Greeley Foundation for Peace and Justice provided funds to convene a multinational group of twenty-five diplomats and scholars who drafted what has come to be called the "Salzburg Initiative"—a series of reforms endorsed by environmental, industry, media and political leaders from more than fifty countries. As a member of this group, I have drawn heavily on the ideas contained in the Salzburg Initiative. In addition, the Salzburg Seminar, a not-for-profit educational center in Austria, hosted seminars in 1990 and 1991 on international environmental negotiation.

These sessions brought together more than one hundred leaders from fifty countries to discuss and debate the merits of possible reforms in the traditional approach to global environmental treaty making. The Salzburg Seminar provides a most extraordinary setting for cross-cultural learning.

My colleagues at the Program on Negotiation at Harvard Law School have, for more than a decade, helped to shape my thinking about the best ways of dealing with differences of all kinds. I have tried to apply their ideas to the unique demands of environmental diplomacy. Bill Breslin offered valuable editorial assistance for which I am very grateful. My students, particularly those enrolled in the MIT International Environmental Negotiation Seminar in 1990, 1991, and 1992 prepared detailed case studies of past environmental treaty-making efforts that have helped me link theory and practice in ways that I could not possibly have achieved on my own.

I believe that no nation should be forced to accept a global agreement that hurts its people more than it helps them, nor to settle for agreements that are painless but fail to reverse past patterns of environmental deterioration. Ultimately, we must slow the rate of environmental change to a pace the biosphere can tolerate. This is the special challenge of environmental diplomacy. I am confident we can do this by improving the processes and strengthening the institutions used to build global consensus. Along the way, we must never lose sight of the fundamental rule of negotiation, even as we focus on the science and the politics of each new environmental threat that emerges: cooperation is possible only when parties with competing interests have an opportunity to generate options for mutual gain.

# CHAPTER 2

# The Weaknesses of the Existing Environmental Treaty-Making System

The complex interactions and procedures by which global environmental agreements are formulated, ratified, and implemented are rarely thought of as a system. But these agreements are, in fact, governed by predictable sets of actors engaged in a relatively structured process of negotiation, constrained by formal and informal rules and customs. The "system," such as it is, exists by default in many cases, and its weaknesses may not be apparent. Before the treaty-making process can be strengthened, we must understand the way this system operates.

The actors in the environmental treaty-making system include governmental leaders, unofficial or nongovernmental interest groups (including environmental action organizations, business associations, and scientific associations), and multilateral entities—particularly agencies of the United Nations such as the United Nations Environment Programme, the World Bank, and the United Nations Development Program. These actors gather information, exchange ideas, formulate proposals, and meet in informal and formal sessions to negotiate, prepare legal documents, and vote whether or not to accept new responsibilities, including taxing themselves to cover the costs of monitoring their global environmental management efforts. They meet periodically to review how well they have done and determine whether or not to take further action.

For the most part, these interactions are guided by the formal rules and informal practices that the United Nations has evolved over several decades. They are also shaped, to a lesser extent, by a body of international law—mostly what is called "soft law"—that reflects commonly accepted norms. Finally, and most important, the treaty-making process is constrained by the global interplay of domestic politics: In the final analysis, only agreements that are politically acceptable to national leaders will be approved.

This complex web of actors, institutions, and practices is always in motion, animated by the efforts of individuals and organizations to advance their interests, selfish or otherwise. Not surprisingly, with all that is going on, it can be difficult to gauge, at any moment, whether or not the system is working well. Indeed, there are serious disagreements about how to measure the success of environmental treaty-making efforts. For those involved directly in treaty negotiations, the signing of formal agreements, after years of debate, seems like a tremendous victory. Yet, for the rest of us, it would be a mistake to measure success in terms of anything less than tangible environmental improvements, regardless of the amount of time or effort it took to hammer out the legal accords.

Many overlapping forces are at work in the biosphere, which makes it difficult to keep track of improvements (and what caused them). Indeed, because of the complexity of natural systems, scientists have great difficulty sorting out which actions account for which outcomes. We are only just beginning to understand global ecological interactions well enough to know exactly how seriously to take some of the threats that currently loom large. So, attributing specific changes to the requirements of particular treaties is almost impossible.

If we cannot attribute improvements to the implementation of specific agreements, how, then, shall we measure the success of global treaty-making efforts? In large part, success is in the eye of the beholder. Those who have strong views about the causes of environmental problems, the remedies that will and will not work, and how responsibility for implementing agreements ought to be assigned see the results of treaty-making efforts in ways that reflect their biases.

Three debates, and where the participants stand on each, account for the most important differences in the ways that the success of international environmental negotiations is gauged. The first is between *pragmatists* and *idealists*. In this debate, both sides are concerned about environmental quality and sustainability, but they have conflicting expectations about what constitutes reasonable progress in the search for fair and efficient solutions to environmental problems. The second debate pits *optimists* versus *pessimists* in what seems like a never-ending battle over how to achieve global cooperation. The optimists and the pessimists are diametrically opposed on both the prospects and the range of global agreements that are possible. The third debate is between *reformers* and *conservatives*. These two groups disagree about the desirability of restructuring the United Nations and the system of multilateral institutions that has evolved since the mid-1940s. Where a person stands on each of these debates frequently determines the extent to which he or she thinks the UN-sponsored, convention-protocol approach to environmental treaty-making is succeeding or failing.

## Knowing How to Measure Success

For some environmental advocates, especially in less economically developed countries, merely getting official representatives together to talk about environmental issues is a sign of great progress. In these countries, little or no attention has been paid to local environmental problems, let alone to global environmental threats. For some environmentalists in these settings, the ones I call pragmatists, almost any effort—no matter how modest—is an important step in the right direction. Agreements can always be strengthened, they argue; the important thing is to get started.

On the other side are the idealists. They worry about treaties that "sound" good but yield few tangible improvements in environmental quality. In their view, these may be worse than no agreement at all. Empty promises, they assert, let politicians off the hook, allowing them to take credit for solving problems when, in fact, the environment may actually be deteriorating at a rapid rate. Indeed, inadequate or partial agreements may forestall the efforts needed to achieve measurable improvement. Thus, the idealists maintain a stringent standard for assessing progress: measurable, documented improvements.

All global efforts to deal with environmental problems ultimately hinge on the willingness of agencies, organizations, and individuals to follow certain rules and, often, to change their behavior. Thus, it is not uncommon to evaluate environmental treaties in terms of the obligations that the signatory states promise to impose upon their industries, citizens, and governments. The pragmatists argue that even purely symbolic statements by a few countries are valuable because they put pressure on reluctant leaders who may be hesitant to make the most modest commitments. The idealists, however, are not satisfied with anything less than full-fledged, enforceable promises to regulate environmentally destructive behavior.

If progress on the environment ultimately depends on the willingness of countries to force citizens and enterprises to live up to tougher standards, the pragmatists argue, then even modest agreements provide support for insurgent environmental protection efforts. It is usually grassroots groups, after all, that shape public perceptions and impose pressure on government leaders to change their policies. On the other hand, if the idealists are right, then the publicity accorded symbolic statements underscoring the need for action (but not requiring any) may actually undermine environmental protection efforts by leading potential supporters within a country to believe that problems have been solved, when indeed they have not.

There are several reasons that signed international agreements (that appeal to the pragmatists) often produce little if any real improvement. First, it often takes so long to secure international cooperation that environmental protection strategies that made sense when they were first proposed represent "too little, too late" by the time they are implemented. The problem may have reached entirely new (and very different) proportions in just a few years. For example, efforts to protect a particular habitat may be irrelevant once a species is extinct.

If too few countries ratify an agreement, the cumulative efforts of those living up to their promises may be insufficient to reverse the problem. It may be impossible, for instance, to clean up the ocean, even if most countries stop dumping toxic wastes, as long as a few countries refuse to halt their dangerous disposal practices.

It often costs more to implement environmental treaties than the signatories anticipated. Although they are listed among the signatories, some countries may actually renege when changing domestic priorities make it impossible for them to live up to their original intentions. Moreover, even after elaborate treaty language has been worked out, disagreements arise over what was intended and what was guaranteed. In the face of such disagreements, disgruntled countries sometimes decide to opt out. Occasionally, disagreements of this sort are nothing more than a cover for a country's change of heart when it discovers the true costs involved or encounters unexpected domestic opposition.

Sometimes, to get countries with significantly different needs or priorities to sign a treaty, a lowest-common-denominator or compromise approach is adopted. Such halfway agreements, not surprisingly, are often insufficient to achieve the intended results. Many times, the objectives of such treaties are laudable, but the programmatic commitments that countries were willing to make could not possibly achieve their espoused objectives.

Thus, even though agreements are signed, the results may be discouraging. Too few countries (or not enough of the right countries) may be involved. In other instances, even though a sufficient number of countries may be supportive at the outset, they sometimes fail to live up to their promises. In still other situations, even when most of the signatories are ready and willing to comply, the problem turns out to be worse than anyone thought, or the problem turns out not to yield to the solutions that were selected. For these reasons, the idealists refuse to count the number of treaties signed or the number of countries signing them as indicators of progress.

The fifteen treaties listed in Table 1 (and further elaborated in Appendix A) are among the most notable examples of global environmental cooperation, although my selection is somewhat arbitrary. The 1991

### Table 1    Name of Treaty

International Convention for the Regulation of Whaling

Antarctic Treaty
  Agreed Measures on the Conservation of Antarctic Fauna and Flora
  Convention for the Conservation of Antarctic Seals
  Convention for the Conservation of Antarctic Marine Living Resources
    (CCAMLR)
  Convention on the Regulation of Antarctic Mineral Resources Activities
    (CRAMRA)
  Protocol on Environmental Protection

Treaty Banning Nuclear Weapons Tests in the Atmosphere, in Outer Space and Underwater

Convention on Wetlands of International Importance Especially as Waterfowl Habitat (RAMSAR)

Convention on the Prevention of Marine Pollution by Dumping of Wastes and Other Matter (London Dumping Convention)

Convention Concerning the Protection of the World Cultural and National Heritage

Convention on International Trade in Endangered Species (CITES)

International Convention for the Prevention of Pollution from Ships (MARPOL)

Convention on the Conservation of Migratory Species of Wild Animals (Bonn)

Convention on Long-Range Transboundary Air Pollution
  Protocol on the Reduction of Sulfur Emissions or their Transboundary Fluxes
    by at least Thirty Percent
  Protocol Concerning the Control of Emissions of Nitrogen Oxides or Their
    Transboundary Fluxes
  Protocol Concerning the Control of Emissions of Volatile Organic Compounds
    or Their Transboundary Fluxes

United Nations Convention on the Law of the Sea (UNCLOS)

Vienna Convention for the Protection of the Ozone Layer
  Montreal Protocol on Substances that Deplete the Ozone Layer

Convention on the Control of Transboundary Movements of Hazardous Wastes and their Disposal (Basel Convention)

Biodiversity Convention

The Convention on Climate Change

UNEP Register of International Treaties and Other Agreements in the Field of the Environment and the 1992 Report of the UNCED Secretariat (entitled *The Effectiveness of International Environmental Agreements*, edited by Peter H. Sand) list more than 120 international agreements and international legal instruments in the environmental field. More than half are regional or sub-regional in scope (and thus are only partially relevant to the study of global agreements). Of the approximately fifty global agreements listed in these two compendiums, about ten are statements of general environmental concerns, eight are concerned with civil liability for environmental damage (from oil spills or nuclear disasters), and another seven are International Labor Organization-sponsored agreements on the protection of workers in the work environment.

Most knowledgeable observers agree that the fifteen global treaties listed in Table 1 have, as yet, failed to reverse the environmental deterioration that they were meant to check (including those signed several decades ago). To be fair, several have slowed the rate of pollution or begun the process of protecting important natural resources, even if they have not repaired past damage. And the last few were signed only in June 1992 (and have not yet come into force).

Consider the dialogue between the idealists and the pragmatists that would take place over the treaties listed in Appendix A. The idealists would argue that most species of whales remain on the verge of extinction (although one or two have made a comeback). Moreover, several whaling nations have recently renewed commercial harvesting of whales after having previously agreed to phase it out. The rate at which wetlands are disappearing is increasing, and most damaged wetlands have not been repaired or replaced. The idealists would probably point out that Antarctica is still not fully protected, and the countries that claim a share of the Antarctic have been unable to agree—even after twenty years of debate and study—on a permanent minerals mining ban. Further, many, if not most, of the significant ecological resources representing "the heritage of mankind" have not been protected from the adverse effects of development. Ocean dumping of toxic and hazardous waste continues while the sludge already at the bottom of the world's oceans has not been retrieved or treated.

From the idealists' standpoint, many endangered species and habitats continue to be lost each year, and there have been few successful efforts to replace those that have been destroyed. The level of hazardous and toxic waste produced each year continues to rise, and increasing volumes are transported from developed to developing nations, creating grave dangers for unsuspecting residents.

The comprehensive Law of the Sea, negotiated for almost ten years, has not yet been (and may never be) ratified by enough countries to take effect. Some of the worst oil spills in history have occurred in recent years with little or no indication of any international cooperation to combat the harmful effects that these accidents have caused. And, although many countries have signed an agreement (called the Montreal Protocol) aimed at protecting the "ozone layer" by banning the use of chlorofluorocarbons (CFCs), a number of key CFC-producing countries have not signed; moreover, other equally damaging emissions, like methane, have not been restricted at all.

Finally, the climate change and biodiversity agreements signed at the Earth Summit in 1992 offer no guarantee that carbon dioxide levels will ever be reduced. In the absence of a treaty on forest protection, important rain forests will continue to be lost. Neither of the treaties signed at the Rio meeting includes specific standards that must be met or deadlines by which signatory countries can be held accountable.

The pragmatists have a very different story to tell. They argue that the fifteen global environmental agreements listed in Appendix A represent dramatic progress. Countries that once paid no attention to natural resource management issues have made explicit commitments to do so. As a result, the environmental movement within each of these countries has been strengthened. The number of whales of all kinds is on the increase, and several have even reached the point where commercial whaling is once again viable. International norms now suggest that it is important to recognize the vital role that wetlands play in maintaining ecological balance. More than 400 wetlands of international importance (comprising almost 30 million hectares—an area the size of Italy) have been preserved. And, the pragmatists would argue, we are closer to achieving a (fifty year) ban on mineral development in Antarctica than we have ever been in the past.

Almost eighty "natural world heritage" sites have been protected, a quarter of them in Africa. Ocean dumping of a number of hazardous and toxic substances has been cut back, and some countries, like the United States, are in the process of phasing out damaging dumping practices all together. Some previously endangered species are no longer facing extinction. There are agreements "on the books" encouraging the reporting and cleanup of oil spills. Migratory flyways are more clearly delineated and some have been protected by countries that previously ignored them.

The pragmatists point out that although the formal Law of the Sea treaty has not yet come into force, many of its provisions have, de facto, been incorporated into international law. Not only have efforts to protect the ozone layer led to a voluntary ban on CFC production in a number of countries but more and more countries are joining the phaseout, as financial arrangements to assist developing nations are finalized. In addition, there is a system in place to keep better track of hazardous wastes transported across national borders. Progress may be slower than some would like, but it is measurable. The fact is, we have climate change and biodiversity agreements that can be strengthened as additional scientific information becomes available.

## Three Serious Obstacles to Global Cooperation

Whether one sides with the pragmatists or the idealists, there are several reasons to be pessimistic about the prospects for achieving the level of cooperation required to manage shared (or common) resources like the oceans, space, Antarctica, the atmosphere, or the diversity of species. The first is the worsening split between the developed nations of the North and the developing nations of the South. The second is the stubborn persistence of national sovereignty as an important goal unto itself. The third is an apparent lack of incentives sufficient to bring some nations to the bargaining table for serious discussions about the nature of global environmental threats and the challenges of sustainable development. The optimists believe that all three of these obstacles can be overcome, making international cooperation possible. The pessimists are doubtful.

## North-South Conflict

The North-South split is often portrayed as a battle over money and technology, but there is more to this conflict than economic and scientific ascendancy. Some observers paint the nations of the South as a supplicant begging for additional aid while the North is portrayed as a wealthy but selfish benefactor unwilling to share its technological secrets. Ever since the 1972 Stockholm Conference on the Human Environment, when the developing nations managed to generate a conference-approved set of principles that challenged prevailing approaches to economic development and environmental protection, the North-South debate has intensified. Often the disagreement revolves around whether funds for the implementation of environmental protection agreements will be added to the development assistance that is already provided to the South ("additionality"), and what (if any) strings the North will attach to these funds ("conditionality"). At the Earth Summit, much attention focused on the issue of technology transfer or technology sharing. U.S. biotechnology firms were worried that the Biodiversity Convention would require them to turn over products they might invent, using materials gathered in the South (even after paying an initial royalty). The South argued for continuing royalties and technology sharing.

The injustice of cultural hegemony (that is, the overwhelming impact of Western culture and the forces of modernization on economically dependent countries) undergirds the development assistance and technology transfer debates. The South wants the North to acknowledge the unfairness of this indirect form of domination. These debates mask the real source of conflict, which is a fundamental difference in how the nations of the North and the South think about progress.

This dichotomy is elegantly presented by Thijs de la Court in *Beyond Brundtland* (1990), in which he describes the Third World's response to the report of the UN World Commission on Environment and Development (otherwise known as the Brundtland Report, after the prime minister of Norway who chaired the commission). The disagreement, as he explains it, is really over the meaning and direction of economic development. Although it may be difficult, particularly for Americans, to believe that most of the developing world—if it had a choice—would prefer not to emulate contemporary Western development patterns, that is indeed the case. To paraphrase two noted Indian critics of the Brundtland Report, there are other ways of defining progress: we need not equate development with economic growth, economic growth with expansion of the market economy, modernity with consumerism, and nonmarket economics with backwardness.[1]

The Brundtland Report (which popularized the idea of sustainable development and postulated the need to link economic development and environmental protection) assumes that effective responses to global environmental threats can be found within the framework of the current pattern of economic development, if only the key actors would accept the importance of sustainability. This is, in fact, the generally held view in the North. The South, however, views its current array of problems (i.e., population growth, food shortages, the loss of forests, the difficulties of producing energy, the impacts of industrialization, and the burdens of massive urbanization) as by-products of the dominant economic development pattern. The South wants the North to accept responsibility for *causing* these problems by pursuing a form of economic growth and an approach to development that is fundamentally at odds with sustainability.

Even though the leaders of many developing nations are currently championing more market-oriented approaches to development and economic growth, they certainly are not seeking to obliterate the unique social, economic, and ecological conditions that make up their cultural identity. In the long run, such a course of action would be (among other things) self-defeating. So, if every nation sought to achieve the levels of per capita energy use and resource consumption currently enjoyed by the United States, the world's reserves would quickly be exhausted. There must be some other pattern of development, therefore, or some fairer way of sharing the world's resources that we ought to pursue instead.

Attitudes toward the World Bank (and other multilateral lending institutions) reflect these contradictory views about what constitutes desirable development. Although the World Bank announced in 1987 its intention to show greater concern for the ecological consequences of its investments than it had in the past (e.g., promising to prepare environmental impact assessments before making future funds available), it did not immediately curtail its support for many large-scale development projects that some in the South see as totally unacceptable. Indeed, the bank's declaration that it would pay more attention to environmental quality was met with harsh skepticism by many Third World environmental action groups that have bitterly opposed bank-financed projects that they feel betray a fundamental blindness to anything other than the North's definition of desirable development.[2]

In Brazil, the World Bank and the Inter-American Development Bank have supported the Palonoroeste Project aimed at opening up virgin tropical forests in the Amazon for new development. In China, the World Bank–financed Three Gorges Dam on the Yangtze River will flood thousands of square miles and force three million people to relocate. In Botswana, the bank has supported large-scale cattle ranching projects that have caused overgrazing of ecologically vulnerable land. The bank's dam and irrigation projects in the Narmada Valley of India have been opposed bitterly by grass-roots groups trying to save their communities. And in Indonesia, the bank has supported the emigration of millions of people to unspoiled areas of other islands in the archipelago. These projects, sometimes referred to as "the fatal five" by critics of the bank, symbolize for many in the developing world the North's continued unwillingness to honor the South's commitment to alternative patterns of development. This, in turn, feeds suspicions that the North's recent statements of concern about environmental quality and sustainability are nothing more than a pretext for further exploitation of the South.[3]

The issues of technology sharing and development aid are far from unimportant, but they are secondary to this larger question. The issue is not how much more money the North will provide to the South, but whether the underlying North-South relationship can be shifted from one of dependence and confrontation to one of fruitful interdependence. In 1986, according to the United Nations and the Organization for Economic Cooperation and Development, the nations of Africa received $18 billion in development assistance. In that same year, the same countries faced $34 billion in losses: $15 billion in loan redemption obligations and $19 billion in export price drops. At the time, Africa's total debt approached $200 billion, a sum that equaled half the continent's overall GNP and three to four times its annual income from exports.[4]

As the Brundtland Report explains: "Debts that they cannot pay force African nations relying on commodity sales to overuse their fragile soils, thus turning good land into desert. Trade barriers in the wealthy nations—and in many developing ones—make it hard for Africans to sell their goods for reasonable returns, putting yet more pressure on ecological systems." What does it matter, then, how much more aid or what kind of technology is made available if the level of dependence only increases and the impact on fragile ecosystems only worsens?

The North-South conflict will not be resolved by doling out additional money or making new technologies available on favorable terms. The South expects the North to accept a greater share of responsibility for the difficulties that developing nations face. The South is also waiting for the North to acknowledge that there must be a change in Northern life-styles if greater fairness in the allocation of the world's resources is to be achieved. From the North's standpoint, neither demand is reasonable. Thus, the deadlock continues, especially because the nations of the South, also called the Group of Seventy-seven (even though there are more than 125 nations in the group), have found their voice and mobilized more effectively in recent years.

## Sovereignty

In March of 1989, at The Hague, the prime ministers of France, Holland, and Norway proposed an ambitious plan to create a global environmental legislative body with the power to impose new environmental regulations and binding legal sanctions on any country that failed to carry them out. The proposal failed, although twenty-four heads of state did adopt a declaration calling for a new United Nations authority empowered to act even without unanimous agreement.[5] From time to time, perhaps more out of frustration than anything else, proposals like this one calling for the creation of supranational bodies with the power to override national sovereignty are put forward. They do not succeed because countries fight desperately to maintain their individual rights and privileges.

Most global environmental agreements worked out through ad hoc negotiations include only weak monitoring and enforcement provisions. This, too, is a function of national efforts to maintain not only control over all decisions within their geopolitical borders but autonomy over actions that affect common areas and resources as well. For example, the International Convention for the Regulation of Whaling established the International Whaling Commission to oversee the provisions of that treaty but failed to give it enforcement powers. So, treaty violations are noted and announced, but sanctions cannot be brought against nations that are in violation. Indeed, if a country is upset about being charged with violations, it can threaten to "opt out" of the agreement or organize a rump group to set competing standards.

Monitoring and enforcement powers are not granted because they appear to conflict with the prerogatives of national sovereignty. Without effective monitoring and enforcement, though, implementation of treaties is difficult. Most countries comply with most existing international agreements, but there are many instances of blatant disregard for rules and deadlines. Sovereignty is often used as an excuse. Countries that find themselves out of compliance assert that the more important issue is that their sovereignty is being undercut by other nations.

One school of international relations holds that because sovereign nations will always act in their own self-interest, international institutions are irrelevant. That is, such institutions will never be able to convince nations to pursue a course of action inconsistent with their self interest.[6] A second school of thought believes that we don't need multilateral institutions because self-interested nations in a competitive setting will always work to achieve mutually beneficial exchanges without any prodding from an international body. As Arthur Stein writes in *Why Nations Cooperate* (1990), "Like a well-functioning market in which self-interested behavior leads to optimal, efficient outcomes, an anarchic international system composed of self-interested states should need no regulation." However, many nations engaged in fairly regular efforts to formulate and implement cooperative arrangements create and empower new institutions to make their collaboration easier. They do this in spite of their desire not to give up their sovereignty.

The international relations theorists notwithstanding, sovereign states seeking to pursue their self-interest often realize that their ability to build and maintain cooperative relationships depends on their capacity to sustain appropriate institutional oversight and assistance. In the same way that communities of people form governments (and in the process give up a measure of autonomy in exchange for security), the nations of the world must, when they come together to work out ways of handling global problems, surrender some degree of sovereignty. The important point, though, is that they do this by choice. And, they can do it in one policy arena while deciding not to do so in another.

The 1982 Law of the Sea Treaty advanced the idea of a "common heritage of mankind" that would have diminished the zone of absolute sovereignty of individual states (i.e., whenever their actions threatened global environmental quality). This was a challenge to the prevailing legal assumption that sovereign states can do whatever they please outside the jurisdictions of other states. Because the Law of the Sea Treaty was not ratified, however, this limit on sovereignty was never adopted.

Of course, many nations long ago accepted other practical limitations on their sovereignty in order to partake of the advantages of international communications and trade. The operation of ports, airlines, telecommunications, and other global systems are all governed by international authorities. As countries find themselves increasingly economically interdependent, their sovereignty diminishes. As new satellite technologies allow global monitoring without direct access to territory, traditional notions of sovereignty are further softened. Nevertheless, while notions of national sovereignty over the management of natural resources (both within a country's borders and in common areas) are evolving in response to technological and economic change, they still pose a substantial obstacle to effective environmental treaty making.

## Incentives to Bargain

Finally, the pessimists are worried (and rightly so) that many nations will refuse to join in global environmental negotiations not because they are worried about losing their sovereignty but because they fail to see what they have to gain. These countries are potential "free riders," (i.e., parties that benefit by the actions of others without sharing any of the responsibility or cost). They assume that others will make enough of an effort so that they will benefit from an environmentally safer world without shouldering any of the costs. Why join the club if you can have all the benefits without any of the costs?

Many of the costs of combating various kinds of pollution must be paid now, although the full range of benefits generated by such pollution control efforts will probably not be realized until well into the next century. This presents a problem for many politicians. Their time horizon runs only until the next election. As with efforts to raise taxes, for example, few elected officials want to be the ones to initiate increases. They all, though, want to share the credit and the benefits when it turns out that the money was well spent. Many environmental treaty negotiations focus only on the allocation of costs (including constraints on development). They devote little or no attention on the tangible benefits that will be generated or how they will be shared.

The impacts of environmental problems and the costs of combating them will almost certainly not be distributed equally. Some countries will lose more than they gain—even in the long run. Unlike other international negotiations, in which the losers are guaranteed benefits of other kinds, loser countries have good reason to remain on the sidelines or even to sabotage international environmental treaty-making efforts. Although linking treaty-making efforts together could change this calculus, it is rarely done. Environmental negotiations have been conducted largely in isolation from negotiations on other international issues such as debt, trade, or security. The complexity of linkage, according to the pessimists, would be beyond the capacity of international institutions to handle.

On balance, these three obstacles—the North-South conflict, the desire to preserve national sovereignty, and the lack of incentives to come to the negotiation table—suggest that the pessimists have good reason to doubt that the future of environmental treaty making is bright. The optimists believe that those deficiencies can be corrected by adjusting the international legal system.

## An Inadequate Legal Structure

The Brundtland Commission recommended the adoption of a universal declaration on environmental protection and sustainable development (see Appendix B) analogous to the Universal Declaration of Human Rights. This was aimed at overcoming one of the most serious inadequacies in the international legal system: the lack of specific national obligations to protect the environment. According to many commentators, particularly Phillipe Sands (director of the Centre of International Environmental Law in London), there are actually two key problems. First, nongovernmental organizations and other "nonstate actors" have no standing in the international legal system (i.e., they are not recognized as legal persons). Only sovereign states are recognized, and they are all equal. It is not likely that one state will be able to prosecute other states on behalf of the global environment, and it is not permitted for nongovernmental actors to assume this prosecutorial role (i.e., negotiate with states and appear before international tribunals). Second, environmental rights have not been established on an international scale. That is what the Brundtland Report was attempting to do.

In the absence of a universal declaration on environmental protection and sustainable development, the Vienna Convention on the Law of Treaties, governing the making of global environmental agreements, provides only process guidelines. The convention spells out some ground rules, although it leaves a great many questions unanswered.[7]

Most multilateral environmental treaty negotiations are initiated by international organizations. In recent years, the UN Environment Programme (UNEP), has been the primary initiator, calling the conferences that produced the Convention on the Ozone Layer in 1985 and the Basel

Convention on the Control of Transboundary Movements of Hazardous Wastes and Their Disposal in 1989. The Earth Summit, while officially under the aegis of a separate UN Conference on Environment and Development, was also a product, at least in part, of UNEP's efforts. Other treaty-making efforts have been stimulated by small groups of countries or international scientific organizations like the International Union for the Conservation of Nature and Natural Resources (IUCN). The Vienna Convention on the Law of Treaties does not specify who should initiate treaty-making efforts.

Some conferences involve only a few countries meeting on a sub-regional basis. Others may involve most of the 180-plus members of the United Nations. Once a conference has been called and the negotiating committees for each nation have convened, they formulate rules regarding how their negotiations will proceed; specifically, how long the conference will last, who will be allowed to participate, who will present scientific evidence, how proposals will be made, and how the participants will formulate the text of an agreement. These rules may be suggested by the international organization that called the conference, or they may have been spelled out in a previous agreement. The Vienna Convention does not specify which countries should participate or how the treaty-making process should proceed. It does say , though, that adoption of the text of a treaty requires "a vote of two-thirds of the states present and voting, unless by the same majority they decide to apply a different rule."

Procedural rules can have a major impact on the chances of reaching agreement. For example, the use of a "single-text" approach, in which there is only one draft of a potential agreement and all parties write their suggested changes on that draft rather than offer alternative versions of the whole text, has been cited by negotiation experts as an important factor in the success of several treaty negotiations. Similarly, the participation of nongovernmental organizations (which often provide technical information to formal delegations) aided in the successful negotiation of the Vienna Convention on the Protection of the Ozone Layer. By contrast, the limited duration of the Basel conference (on the transport of hazardous substances) has been cited as a reason that its treaty was unacceptable to some of the nations involved. The Vienna Convention on the Law of Treaties neither suggests nor rules out a single text procedure. It offers no suggested timetable for negotiations. It also fails to address the issue of roles for nongovernmental organizations because, as already mentioned, such groups have no standing in international law.

Once the parties have adopted the text of an agreement, the next step is to secure signatures. For sub-regional conferences involving a relatively small number of parties, each country normally signs at the conclusion of the conference. For larger regional and global conferences, agreements usually "remain open for signature" for an extended period of time at one or more locations. For example, the Vienna Convention on the Protection of the Ozone Layer was open for signature in Vienna for six months and then in New York for six months. Sometimes agreements remain open for signature indefinitely. This was the case with the Convention on Wetlands of International Importance Especially as Waterfowl Habitat (RAMSAR).

Signature is not a trivial step because parties unhappy with the adopted text of an agreement may refuse to sign it. This is especially true when a text is adopted by majority vote rather than by consensus. Once a party signs an agreement it must—according to the Vienna Convention on the Law of Treaties—refrain from activities that would defeat the objectives of the agreement. There are no sanctions prescribed for countries that violate this requirement.

The Vienna Convention provides that an agreement take effect, or enter into force, when a sufficient number of parties have agreed to be bound by it. For most multilateral agreements, the parties can choose to have the agreement enter into force when a fraction of the states have indicated that their governments have ratified it. For regional agreements involving a relatively small number of parties, agreements usually enter into force when all parties have ratified it. Large regional and global agreements typically set a minimum number of required ratifications. The Climate Change Convention, for example, will enter into force when fifty of the 153 signatory countries ratify it. The Biodiversity Convention requires only thirty of the 152 signatories to ratify. The RAMSAR agreement is an exception; it entered into force when seven nations became parties but allowed other nations to become signatories later. Once the minimum number of ratifications is achieved, the agreement enters into force only for those parties who ratify. There is no requirement, according to the Vienna Convention on the Law of Treaties, that a minimum number of countries participate in a treaty-making effort.

Multilateral agreements can be modified after they enter into force. Unless a treaty stipulates otherwise, the general rule is that all signatories must be notified of any proposed modifications. The parties then have the right to participate in modification negotiations, and to sign any subsequent agreement.

Although most multilateral agreements follow this pattern, there are exceptions. Some modifications may be binding on all parties to the original agreement. In such cases, a supermajority vote is usually required for the modification to be adopted. For example, the Vienna Ozone Convention allows any party to propose new amendments. It requires the parties to make "every effort" to reach agreement by consensus, but if they fail, the amendment may be adopted "as a last resort" by a three-fourths majority vote of the parties at the conference.

A typical treaty, or convention agreement, has a predictable set of headings or sections (see Table 2). Most begin with articles defining the key terms used in the agreement and specifies its geographic scope. Next, there are articles calling on the parties to take "all appropriate measures" to address the problem, cooperate with one another in promoting scientific research, share information, deal with emergencies, and carry out the other provisions of the agreement. Sometimes the agreement expressly calls for the parties to formulate specific accords, or protocols, on each of these items. In such cases, the convention outlines the provisions for establishing protocols.

Additional articles usually call for periodic meetings or follow-up conferences. At these meetings, delegates review new scientific information and establish additional research objectives; they assess the effectiveness of the individual and joint measures taken to combat the problem; and propose, discuss, and vote on additional protocols and amendments. Such meetings typically occur once every few years. "Extraordinary" meetings may be called at the request of a predetermined number of parties (sometimes one-third, sometimes half the signatories).

Other articles establish a secretariat (although the Vienna Convention on the Law of Treaties does not specify who should play this role). The primary duty of the secretariat is to call and supervise meetings. Additional responsibilities of the secretariat include transmitting information submitted by one party to the others, ensuring coordination with other international organizations, performing any functions assigned to it in the protocols, and preparing reports about its activities. The secretariat is usually an international organization such as UNEP.

Proposed protocols or amendments to a treaty must be submitted to the secretariat well in advance of regular meetings. The secretariat then sends them to the other parties several months before the next scheduled meeting. At these sessions, the parties try to reach agreement by consensus, but if they fail, amendments can be adopted by a vote of those present. Most amendments to the conventions listed in Table 1 and Appendix A usually focus on what is listed in annexes or appendices to the formal documents. These include technical definitions and actions appropriate to various special circumstances. For example, the annexes to the 1973 Convention on International Trade in Endangered Species of Wild Flora and Fauna (CITES) indicate which species are accorded various levels of protection. The annexes to the London Dumping Convention categorize various substances that may or may not be disposed of in the ocean.

## Table 2  Elements of a Typical Global Environmental Convention

Definitions
  Key terms defined

Objective

Principles
  Needs and rights

Commitments
  Categorization of countries for purposes of implementation; timetables,
    targets, task coordination, financing obligations

Research and Systematic Observation
  Data collection, binding nature, international efforts to strengthen capacity,
    special efforts in developing countries

Education, Training, and Public Awareness
  Within signatory countries, international cooperation

Conference of the Parties
  Establishment, activities, decision making, convening, membership

Secretariat
  Designation and functions

Subsidiary Body for Scientific and Technological Advice
  Establishment, functions, responsibilities

Financial mechanisms
  Assignment of financial responsibility, operational oversight and
    accountability, mechanisms for financial transfers including technology
    transfer, relationship to other bilateral, regional, and multilateral channels

Communication of Information Related to Implementation
  Obligation to communicate with other parties and the secretariat, timing of
    required communications

Resolution of Questions Regarding Implementation
  Multilateral consultative process

Settlement of Disputes
  Obligations of the parties, hierarchy of methods of dispute resolution,
    institutional arrangements, procedures for utilization

Amendments to the Convention
  Procedures, decision rules

Adoption and Amendment of Annexes to the Convention
  Procedures, decision rules

Protocols
  Procedures for adoption, entry into force, acceptable parties, and their
    participation

Right to Vote
  Assignment of voting rights

(*continued*)

**Table 2** *(Continued)*

Depository
  Designation

Signature
  Location and timetable for signing

Interim Arrangements
  Assignment of responsibility for secretarial function, monitoring, and
    financial operations

Ratification, Acceptance, Approval, or Accession
  Timing, binding nature, extent of competence

Entry into Force
  Timing, numbers required

Reservations
  Whether allowed or not

Withdrawal
  Timing and terms

Authentification of Texts
  Languages required

Annexes

Finally, most treaties contain articles defining how they will enter into force. Other articles determine when and how long the agreement will remain open for signature. Another will designate a depository whose duties are to receive notices of ratification and rejection and, when enough parties have ratified, to inform the governments involved. The depository is usually the government of the nation that hosted the meeting at which the convention was signed. Further articles can specify the number of countries that must ratify for an agreement to enter into force, and how long the agreement is expected to remain in force (usually indefinitely).

The reformers look at this legal structure and see glaring weaknesses: the rules are very sketchy; no one is really in charge; much of the negotiation process is ad hoc and unregulated; there is no central authority to manage the process or compel compliance; and the dispute resolution mechanisms available through the International Court of Justice are not definitive. Conservatives, as I call them, view the treaty-making apparatus and nod approvingly: there is no overbearing bureaucracy telling countries what they must do; the fact that procedures are sketched only in broad-brush strokes means that it is relatively easy to make whatever adjustments are needed; and most countries seem to be in compliance most of the time.

The contrast between these two views can be traced to the very different levels of confidence that reformers and conservatives have in the mechanisms for making and enforcing international law. According to the noted legal scholar Patricia Birnie, international law can be developed either by treaty, by custom, or by reference to general principles.[8] Treaties are clear; customs are not. Custom, in international law, refers to practices that provide concrete evidence of a country's willingness to abide by certain rules. General principles of law are contained in the decisions of national and international tribunals. In addition, scholarly writings shape their interpretation. UN General Assembly resolutions and the resolutions of other UN bodies and conferences also shape world opinion about general principles of law.

The accommodation of interests by diplomacy has given rise to a legal order, even though there is no centralized legislative body that formulates or enforces international law. The reformers want a more explicit supranational system with the power to legislate and coerce uncooperative states; the conservatives not only hold out no such hope but oppose all efforts to eliminate sovereignty as we know it.

Because states are sovereign, their consent, or at least their acquiescence, is required to develop international law. Birnie suggests that acquiescence may be assumed if states do not protest at critical junctures, when new customs are crystallized, but this does not speak to the issue of compliance or enforcement. The International Court of Justice provides a dispute resolution mechanism that can sometimes be called into play, but it has no power to coerce a country that refuses to accept its jurisdiction or judgments. In sum, the international legal structure provides very few and very modest guidelines to regulate global environmental treaty making.

## Fundamental Flaws in the Convention-Protocol Approach

Most recent international environmental negotiations have followed a two-step approach. An initial series of meetings is held to review scientific evidence and draft a framework convention. Then, subsequent meetings of the signatories focus on the preparation of detailed protocols. The convention-protocol approach has produced a number of agreements (see Appendix A), the Climate Change Convention and the Biodiversity Convention being the most recent examples of first-step agreements. The Montreal Protocol is the best-known example of what the second step in the two-step process is supposed to generate.

The Vienna Convention on Substances that Deplete the Ozone Layer was signed by twenty-one countries in 1985, eight years after the initial meetings were held to review scientific evidence concerning ozone depletion. The Montreal Protocol was signed two years later by twenty-seven countries, and took effect in 1989. The protocol was revised in 1990 at the first four-year review session in London. The signatories decided to amend the targets and timetables they had set earlier, and took up the question (again) of how to provide sufficient assistance to the nations of the South to enable them to meet the terms of the protocol.

The convention-protocol approach allows countries to "sign on" at the outset even if there is no agreement on the specific actions that must be taken. The 1975 Barcelona Convention (a regional agreement that produced the Mediterranean Action Plan) established procedures for monitoring various sources of pollution without ordering specific pollution controls or reduction levels. Most countries could agree that further documentation of pollution levels would be desirable, but commitments to specific targets would have been difficult for some countries to accept because of domestic opposition to the short-term economic consequences. Nevertheless, the signing of this and other conventions created momentum and encouraged a commitment to continued scientific inquiry.[9]

The 1992 Climate Change Convention sets no targets or timetables (even though many countries, particularly the Europeans, wanted them). Instead, subsequent meetings will consider the results of ongoing scientific inquiries and explore the possibility of adopting specific implementation measures. In the meantime, some nations have unilaterally adopted timetables and targets that affect only themselves. Although these are not legally binding (that is, subsequent legislatures in those countries are free to abrogate them), they provide a benchmark for subsequent negotiations and may give the countries that have taken action the upper hand in negotiations over follow-up protocols in that they can declare that the standards they have already adopted should become the norm.

Groups within countries concerned about environmental protection have been able to point to the signing of framework conventions as proof that further action is still required. In some cases, the accumulation of scientific evidence (made possible by the signing of a convention) will be sufficient to melt political resistance to remedial actions. In other instances, the force of world opinion, stimulated in part by the signing of a convention, has been sufficient to pressure reluctant countries to sign agreements. Sometimes, with the mere passage of time, domestic opposition has weakened, making it easier for national leaders to build support for the actions outlined in follow-up protocols.

A major shortcoming of the convention-protocol approach, however, is that it encourages a process that is often long and drawn out. The 1973 CITES Convention was not signed until ten years after the IUCN first called attention to the need for an international effort to regulate the export, transit, and importation of endangered animal and plant species and their products. During that decade, many animal and plant species were destroyed. Likewise, the Law of the Sea negotiations took ten years, during which time opportunities to preserve and develop maritime resources were lost.

Often the dynamics of the convention-protocol approach reinforce the tendency to seek lowest-common-denominator agreements. The Basel Convention on the Control of Transboundary Movements of Hazardous Wastes and Their Disposal, for instance, incorporated vague language and avoided the politically difficult task of defining key terms. This made it possible for reluctant countries to sign but undermined the chances of successful implementation. Indeed, the developing nations of Africa met in 1991 to sign a regional accord called the Bamaco Agreement, going far beyond the terms of the Basel Convention, to ban the importation of hazardous waste by African countries. The Basel Convention calls for the disposal of hazardous waste in an "environmentally sound manner," but it does not say what this means. The standard of environmental soundness is left entirely up to each country. The Bamaco Agreement was an effort on the part of some African nations to postulate tougher environmental standards.

In a 1989 meeting of the signatories to the CITES Convention, the group agreed to recategorize the African elephant, shifting it to a list requiring more stringent protection. The proposal was resisted by certain ivory-trading nations and was accepted only after a provision was added allowing individual countries to petition for a "downlisting" of the African elephant from endangered to threatened. The criteria for determining the appropriateness of downlisting were not specified in the regulations. In the final analysis, this might well thwart the effectiveness of the treaty.

Most international environmental treaties impose the same requirements on all signatories. Indeed, that is why the lowest-common-denominator solution is often the only viable option. The Basel Convention regulates the movement of hazardous wastes between signatory countries but allows for bilateral agreements between signatory countries and nonsignatory countries. This explicitly contradicts an earlier provision of the agreement that states that signatory countries cannot ship hazardous wastes to nonsignatory countries. The provision allowing bilateral agreements can certainly be interpreted as a watering down of the overall treaty; however, its inclusion was politically necessary to hold the agreement together. Obviously, all treaty negotiations require a give-and-take among countries. In the case of environmental agreements, however, merely satisfying the political demands of the countries involved is not enough. The dynamics of the natural systems involved must be respected, regardless of the political implications.

Another key problem is that agreements produced by the convention-protocol approach sometimes reflect an outright neglect of available scientific and technical information. They sometimes incorporate requirements that turn out to be technically infeasible or illogical. In negotiating a pollution control strategy for the Mediterranean, for example, political considerations overshadowed the technical wisdom of including the Black Sea states of Bulgaria and Romania. According to Peter Haas, author of *Saving the Mediterranean* (1991), a regional agreement was made to satisfy political pressures even though all the parties involved knew they were doing the wrong thing from the standpoint of common sense.

Unfortunately, when it comes time to work out specific second-step protocols, the terms of the original convention can get in the way of producing technically appropriate agreements. Some observers have noted that U.S. support for regulating CFCs was first constrained, and later facilitated, by the development of CFC substitutes by Dupont Chemical Corporation, the major CFC producer in the United States. During convention negotiations, countries will often cite scientific evidence that justifies the general policies they prefer. Because the implications of these policies need not be confronted at that point, counterproductive policies, which frequently constrain subsequent protocol design, may be adopted. This is a very real danger of the two-step drafting process.

Finally, negotiations that occur through the convention-protocol process are often dominated by the most powerful states. The final deal leading to the Montreal Protocol was negotiated primarily between the United States and the European Economic Community, the two largest consumers and producers of CFCs. The developing world was kept on the sidelines. African states have called the Basel Convention a "sellout" by Third World signatories because of the inability of the weaker states to win inclusion of provisions shifting the liability for hazardous waste disposal from recipient states to the generating or exporting states.

The ad hoc nature of the convention-protocol approach to treaty making is partly to blame. In the absence of a formal negotiation system spelling out the rights of each country to help set agendas and the obligations of the secretariat to achieve a certain minimum threshold of support from UN members before environmental treaties can be considered, the most powerful states can, in effect, write the rules, control the dissemination of technical information, and dominate the negotiation process.

The ad hoc convention-protocol approach as currently practiced also fails to come to grips with important negotiation problems. For example, the convention-protocol approach actually encourages the "hard-bargaining" tendencies of many countries in the sense that it does little to discourage countries from misrepresenting their interests. It is not designed to encourage countries to separate the tasks of "creating options for mutual gain" from the task of securing agreement. Furthermore, it focuses insufficient attention on building informal agreements and coalitions prior to formal meetings. These are well-known negotiation problems that contribute to the difficulties of all multilateral negotiations.[10]

Countries often misrepresent or exaggerate their needs as part of their bargaining strategy. This tactic may be useful in one-shot, single-issue negotiations; however, in circumstances where long-term working relationships are crucial to implementation, the parties involved are better off if they make only statements that turn out to be true. This leads to greater trust, which makes implementation easier. In addition, when negotiators are in the business of trading concessions (rather than engaging in a search for trades that maximize joint gains), they must keep checking back with their leaders at home. Very little creativity is possible under these circumstances. An inordinate amount of time is wasted performing the "concessionary dance." In sum, when negotiations involve many issues and many parties who will have to deal with one another on a continuing basis, it makes more sense to share candid accounts of each side's interests and avoid positional bargaining. There is nothing in the two-step approach to environmental treaty making that pushes the parties in this direction.

When negotiations are conducted without a clear separation between creating multiple options for dealing with specific issues and choosing among them, negotiators usually fail to explore the full range of possibilities. A willingness to explore options, or what mediators often call "supposals," is too often misconstrued as a commitment because the parties fail to distinguish "inventing" from "committing," as Roger Fisher, William Ury, and Bruce Patton suggest in *Getting to Yes* (second edition, 1991). This inhibits creative problem solving. All too often, negotiations become a test of will. When they do, parties lock into a battle over a small number of options, which closes down creative brainstorming (that might yield additional alternatives responsive to the interests of all).

The two-step structure of the convention-protocol approach makes no distinction between the tasks of inventing and committing, although it could. At the convention-writing stage, the goal is typically to stay at a very general level so that all countries will at least agree that some (unspecified) action is needed to solve a problem. At the protocol-writing stage, the goal is usually to find a formula that everyone can accept. Such formulas typically contain a great many exceptions, underscoring the fact that no country can be forced to sign. Convention and protocol writing are usually treated as zero-sum games; that is, everyone acts as if anything good for one country must be bad for another. By the time countries have come together to negotiate treaty language, they have usually locked into positions. When agreements do emerge, they are usually the result of compromise by the most powerful parties rather than the result of creative resolution of differences.

In many of the examples cited above, the agenda for each negotiation was set through informal communication between the secretariat or lead organization and a few dominant nations. For example, in the meetings of the International Whaling Commission, the agenda was rigidly controlled by the whaling nations for many years. Certainly, in negotiations in which each nation knows its self-interest, the agenda should be crafted to ensure that the issues of greatest concern to affected states are included. If important issues are omitted, some nations will have no incentive to participate, or they may feel compelled to sabotage the negotiations or subsequent implementation of agreements. However, a more flexible and inclusive approach to agenda setting for treaty negotiation is needed. Unfortunately, the narrowing of negotiations that occurs when specific protocols are debated one at a time, and the general formula is already set by a signed framework convention push environmental treaty negotiations in exactly the wrong direction.

The convention-protocol approach to international environmental negotiations as currently practiced also fails to take account of the special qualities of environmental problems. Many negotiations tend to focus solely on allocating losses or costs incurred through environmental regulation but do not deal with the gains resulting from wiser resource management, or the ways in which these gains might be shared. Indeed, most environmental treaties aim to curtail pollution or regulate the use of common resources by restricting the activities of participating countries. The economic losses suggested by these new rules provide solid excuses for many nations not to join the negotiations. Ways of sharing the economic and ecological benefits of environmental protection are rarely offered as a compelling rationale for participation, although the gains really ought to be the focus, not the losses.

In addition, environmental issues almost invariably involve a degree of scientific uncertainty that complicates decision making. Our understanding of the natural world is incomplete. Forecasting tools provide only crude approximations based on often unverifiable assumptions. Disagreement among technical experts on complex environmental issues is pervasive. If one country thinks it will be disadvantaged by a particular policy proposal, it can easily locate sympathetic experts to raise doubts about the adequacy of the scientific evidence put forward by others. If a country wants to delay implementation of costly pollution abatement measures, it is not hard to argue that further study would be desirable before long-term commitments are made. At the same time, the dynamics of environmental deterioration are hard to reverse. Even if there were an immediate 100 percent cut in ozone depleters worldwide, for instance, it would still take approximately sixty years for chlorine concentrations in the atmosphere to come down to their 1985 levels. It is also worth pointing out, as certain environmental advocacy groups have, that 1985 levels were the levels that permitted the hole in the ozone layer to occur![11]

Many environmental issues also hinge on the problem of how best to manage a common resource, or its converse, how to penalize "free riders"—the beneficiaries of environmental improvements who refuse to pay for or help achieve them. If the benefits of regulated development or pollution control are diffuse, and accrue to all nations irrespective of their behavior, some nations will feel little or no incentive to accept any restrictions. For example, nations such as India have refused to sign the Montreal Protocol. Reductions in the use and production of CFCs by other nations (especially bigger users) will slow down the rate of ozone depletion, and India, as well as the rest of the world, will benefit. The tragedy, however, is that if most countries took this stand, it would never be possible to curb ozone depletion. There is nothing about the convention-protocol approach as currently practiced that solves the free-rider problem or motivates collective action.

Environmental negotiations, up to now, have been conducted largely in isolation from negotiations on other international issues such as debt, trade, or security. Negotiations sponsored solely by UNEP cannot speak to linkages between environmentally related actions and other important economic and security-related considerations. Recently, some developing nations have raised the desirability of making these linkages, particularly between environmental protection and international trade. Environmental scientists, certainly, wish that linkages among different environmental problem-solving efforts could be made more explicit. What ecologists call a "cross-media approach" is necessary to ensure that the solutions to one problem do not merely shift the risk or the impact to another domain (where the effects might even be worse).

Finally, the convention-protocol approach as currently practiced fails to respond to the need for effective monitoring and enforcement. Most environmental agreements worked out through ad hoc international negotiations include only weak monitoring and enforcement provisions. Almost every agreement listed in Appendix A relies on self-reporting and self-enforcement. Monitoring and enforcement are difficult because they conflict, as was pointed out earlier, with the prerogatives of national sovereignty. Yet, without effective monitoring and enforcement, implementation of any agreement is difficult. Although it is true that there is a relatively high rate of compliance with most of the terms of most international treaties, it does not take much noncompliance to undermine the effectiveness of a treaty. And, there has certainly been noncompliance with many global environmental treaties.[12] All of these weaknesses were clearly in evidence in the Earth Summit negotiations.

## The Earth Summit as an Illustration

The 1972 Stockholm Conference on the Human Environment marked an important turning point. Before 1972, separate UN agencies dealt with environmental problems on a piecemeal basis. After Stockholm, the United Nations moved to coordinate its environmental activities through the creation of the United Nations Environment Programme, or UNEP. UNEP is not an executive agency. It is not financed or empowered to carry out its own programs. Instead, it depends on other national and international agencies to implement the programs it helps to design. Along with the Brundtland Commission and a variety of other international organizations, UNEP encouraged the United Nations General Assembly (in 1989) to create the United Nations Conference on the Environment and Development, or UNCED. The UNCED charter declared: "The Conference should elaborate strategies and measure to halt and reverse the effects of environmental degradation in the context of strengthened national and international efforts to promote sustainable and environmentally sound development in all countries."

As late as 1991, the major results of the Earth Summit were expected to be four signed conventions on climate change, biological diversity, biotechnology, and forests (down from seven as originally mandated); a charter of planetary rights defining basic guidelines for balancing environmental protection and economic development (otherwise known as an "Earth Charter"); a plan of action for setting the planet on a path toward sustainable development in the twenty-first century (Agenda 21); a redefinition of roles and responsibilities for various UN agencies; agreement on the financial mechanisms needed to implement Agenda 21; and a general agreement on technology transfer.

Three working groups were established by the UNCED Secretariat, headed by a Canadian, Maurice Strong (who also headed the Stockholm Conference). The first working group was chaired by a Swede, Ambassador Bo Kjellen. It focused on protection of the atmosphere (i.e., climate change, depletion of the ozone layer, and transboundary air pollution); protection and management of land resources (i.e., deforestation, desertification, drought, and land degradation); conservation of biological diversity; and environmentally sound management of biotechnology. The second working group was headed by Dr. Bukar Shaib of Nigeria. It, too, had an ambitious agenda: protection of oceans, seas, and coastal areas, and the planned use of their living resources; protection of the supply and quality of fresh water resources; environmentally sound management of hazardous wastes and the prevention of illegal international traffic in toxic waste and other dangerous products; environmentally sound management of toxic chemicals; and improvement of the living and working environment of the poor, protection of human health conditions, and improvement in the quality of life. The third working group was chaired by Bedrich Moldan from the former Czechoslovakia. This group (which was not established until almost a year after the first two) was responsible for the legal, financial, and institutional framework for an "Earth Charter" and Agenda 21. In addition, the third working group had responsibility for such cross-cutting questions as the financing of international programs; removing barriers to technology transfer; design of new legal institutions and instruments; possible reforms in the organization of the UN agency structure; economic instruments like pricing policies, tradable permits, national economic accounting systems, and fiscal incentives; penalties to encourage enforcement; and supporting measures like information management, training, and public education.

Four preparatory meetings (PrepComs) were held. The PrepCom membership was drawn from the 150-plus national delegations committed to participating in the Earth Summit. Many delegates were drawn from missions based in Geneva (because of the UNCED Secretariat's location there) and New York, site of the General Assembly. Delegations also included national technical experts. Nongovernmental organizations participated both as part of national delegations and as official observers.

The first PrepCom in Nairobi, Kenya, in August 1990, resulted in a request to the UNCED Secretariat to prepare eighty (later reduced to thirty) background reports. There was a great deal of wrangling over the role that nongovernmental organizations should be allowed to play in UNCED's deliberations. At the second PrepCom in Geneva, in March 1991, another fifty reports were requested. This avalanche of requests was an indication that the PrepCom participants were unprepared to deal with the difficult issues that had been put before them.[13] The principal achievement of PrepCom II was the creation of Working Group III.

PrepCom III was held in August 1991, in Geneva, and was much more successful. There was agreement that there should be an Agenda 21. Most of the countries present supported the idea of an "Earth Charter." A preliminary statement of general principles on the protection of the world's forests was also approved.

PrepCom IV was held just before the Earth Summit, in March 1992, in New York. Although the session snagged on the question of financial resources, those present adopted and sent along to the Rio conference a draft of Agenda 21. On the final day of PrepCom IV, the Group of Seventy-seven broke off negotiations on a financing plan, leaving the specifics to the negotiators in Rio.

The Group of Seventy-seven was working from a draft on finances prepared by China and Pakistan. It called for "adequate, new and additional funds, covering the full incremental costs with no reallocation of existing multilateral or bilateral financial flows" to finance Agenda 21 activities by developing countries. The Group of Seventy-seven also wanted a special fund for the implementation of Agenda 21 that would (1) be in addition to official development assistance already targeted to developed countries; (2) require mandatory contributions from developed countries; (3) give equal voice to all parties in determining project eligibility criteria, project selection, and the release of funds; and (4) fund activities according to the priorities and needs of the developing countries.[14] Not surprisingly, the industrialized countries bracketed all of these demands and offered alternatives on each point. The PrepCom chair, Tommy Koh of Singapore, directed a small group to try to work something out but, after two weeks of behind-closed-door meetings, there was no progress. Koh then tried to formulate a compromise, but it, too, fell apart when the European Community insisted that only the Global Environmental Facility (GEF)—a temporary creation of the World Bank, UNEP, and the United Nations Development Programme (UNDP)—should allocate the funds to implement Agenda 21.

The Principles on World Forests were drafted by the PrepCom, but the Climate Change Conventions and Biodiversity Convention were prepared independently by Intergovernmental Negotiating Committees established several years earlier by UNEP. Subcommittees involving representatives from more than one hundred countries struggled to find treaty language that would be acceptable at Rio.

When the actual Earth Summit was finally held in Rio de Janeiro in early June 1992, more heads of state were in attendance than at any previous UN conference on any subject, although not for the full two weeks. U.S. President Bush held off deciding whether to attend until just a month before the conference, unconvinced that the interests of the United States would be well served but worried about the impact of nonattendance on his standing in the presidential election. Numerous resolutions were introduced in the U.S. House and the Senate, not only calling on the president to attend but spelling out—in no uncertain terms—U.S. support for the strongest possible versions of all the treaties scheduled for discussion.

In the end, Bush attended, but for just three days. The United States was roundly criticized in the world press when the president refused to sign the Biodiversity Convention. The United States was also criticized when, at the last minute, Bush tried to push his own version of a forest protection treaty. He failed to commit substantial new and additional development assistance, and, in general, played no visible leadership role.

The conference was not able to agree on an "Earth Charter" establishing new legal rights or responsibilities relative to environmental protection or sustainable development. The final version of the Rio Statement calls on all countries to do everything possible to promote sustainable development but breaks no new ground on this subject.

Although the United States refused to sign the Biodiversity Convention, 153 other countries did. The convention calls for all countries to prepare policies, programs, and plans to conserve and protect biological diversity. Each signatory is supposed to do everything it can to ensure access to its genetic resources as well as to technologies ("for sustainable use of biological diversity") that will help the other signatories. The developing nations are promised the full increment of aid required to meet the terms of the treaty (although amounts are not specified and mechanisms for distribution must be worked out at a later date).

The United States agreed to sign the Climate Change Convention, but only after it was watered down substantially. Just months before the Earth Summit, the European Community was adamant that it would not support a climate change convention that did not include mandated targets and timetables for reductions in the emission of greenhouse gases. (Many European nations had already adopted substantial carbon dioxide reductions on their own.) It is not clear how the United States maneuvered the Europeans into changing their stand, especially because many Group of Seventy-seven members were quite willing to isolate the United States by proceeding with a treaty that the United States could not sign.

The Climate Change Convention calls on all countries to do all they can to mitigate climate change by reducing or preventing the emission of greenhouse gases, promoting sustainable development, cooperating in preparing for adaptation to the impacts of climate change, and exchanging relevant scientific information. The North is called upon to "adopt national policies and take corresponding measures on the mitigation of climate change, by limiting its anthropogenic emissions of greenhouse gases and protecting and enhancing its greenhouse gas sinks and reservoirs." Again, the developed countries promised to provide the South with "new and additional financial resources to meet the agreed full costs incurred in complying with the treaty." Presumably, as additional scientific evidence becomes available to support the claim that global warming is indeed occurring, and with the reports in hand required by the Climate Change

Convention, it will be possible to specify timetables and targets in subsequent protocols.

A great deal of attention at Rio was focused on the level of aid that the North would provide to help implement Agenda 21 and the two conventions. (There was no agreement on a forest treaty or a treaty on desert expansion.) Maurice Strong announced before the start of the Earth Summit that it might take as much as $125 billion a year to implement Agenda 21. It was not clear how much new money was actually promised at Rio, but even the most optimistic total falls far short of Strong's estimate. The developing world uses 0.7 percent of Gross National Product as an overseas development assistance target for the nations of the North. A few Northern countries accept this goal, although very few have actually met it; most, including the United States, still do not endorse this target. (The financial details of the Rio agreement, and the related issues of additionality and conditionality of aid are discussed in later chapters.)

The money that the North promised will flow, in large part, through the Global Environmental Facility (GEF), even though the Group of Seventy-seven was not entirely happy about this. Some accommodation was made to the South when the organizers of the GEF (the World Bank, the UNDP, and UNEP) agreed to change its administrative structure somewhat to ensure more of a role for the South in making allocation decisions. This was a response to the charge that the United States (through its supposedly disproportionate control over the World Bank) had too much say over GEF allocations in developing countries. The issue of control remains unsettled.

Agenda 21 grew longer and longer as the Earth Summit preparations proceeded. By the time everyone had finished adding to it, the document was almost eight hundred pages in length and included more than forty chapters plus appendices. It is not really an agenda for action because it contains no priorities of any kind.

The results of the Earth Summit and the events preceding it offer conclusive evidence of the weaknesses of the existing environmental treaty-making system. There was, after all, no international agreement on the range or content of the environmental threats that had to be addressed. UNEP, and then the UNCED Secretariat determined the process rules; others went along. There was little or no philosophical agreement on the types of solutions likely to be most effective, or even on the most efficient ways of allocating responsibility for implementation.

The idealists would say that the Earth Summit failed miserably because no ironclad commitments were made to reverse or repair environmental deterioration. Rio did not produce responses to many of the serious environmental threats we now face. The pragmatists would say, though, that substantial progress was made: two framework conventions were signed, and there were resolutions adopted on a great many other issues, denoting a new level of international attention to problems that must be recognized before collective action is possible. Additional funding was promised by the North, and a great deal of public attention was focused on the idea of sustainable development.

Although North-South differences did not block all action, they certainly bounded the debate and made it impossible for the United States to sign the Biodiversity Convention. Almost nothing was done to strengthen multilateral institutions with global environmental management responsibilities. There was agreement to create the United Nations Commission on Sustainable Development, but its powers will be extremely limited. No new law was written—nothing like an Earth Charter or the earlier Brundtland Sustainable Development Declaration was enacted. We will have to wait several more years to see whether follow-up protocols on climate change and biodiversity are enacted, and whether there will be full-fledged forest and desert treaties.

We certainly can consider the agreements reached at Rio as lowest-common-denominator results. The countries involved politicized the search for scientific understanding, engaging in some of the worst adversary science ever seen. They minimized the search for creative options by focusing narrowly rather than broadly on the full range of environment and development issues requiring attention. They undervalued the importance of benefit sharing, focusing more on short-term economic costs than on long-term environmental gains for future generations. There were no innovative proposals for ensuring compliance or dealing with free-rider nations. The final results were dominated by the most powerful states, while nongovernmental interests were left to formulate unofficial treaties at the parallel Global Forum for nongovernmental organizations.

I am certain that the system that produced such modest results at UNCED can be strengthened, even in the face of worldwide recession, continued North-South hostility, and a fierce determination to preserve national sovereignty. In the four chapters that follow, I will point out how politically acceptable improvements might be made.

# CHAPTER 3

# Representation and Voting

What are the incentives for national governments to participate in global environmental treaty-making efforts? And, why is the United Nations resistant to offering nongovernmental organizations a more full-fledged role in the treaty-making process? These questions could be addressed separately, but I believe they are intrinsically related. Both deal with representation—who is at the negotiation table—and that issue is often the most conflictual in any environmental discussion.

Since its founding, the United Nations has been an organization comprising governments, just fifty-one at first, but now more than 180. According to its charter, it's primary objective is to maintain international peace and security, but the organization has other goals as well, including "the development of friendly relations among nations, the achievement of international cooperation in solving international economic, social, cultural, and humanitarian problems; and harmonizing the actions of nations in their efforts to attain their common ends."

According to Article Two of the UN Charter, certain principles must be observed: all members are sovereign and equal; disputes must be resolved peaceably; members are expected to support the organization in its efforts to achieve the goals stated in its Charter; and the United Nations is not to intervene (except in cases of enforcement) in the domestic affairs of any country. The Charter assumes that the United Nations is an organization of states, and even though nongovernmental organizations play an advisory, or informal, role in its operation, they have been given no formal role in UN decision making.

There are—at times—significant benefits for national governments to participate in environmental treaty making, benefits that often transcend any obligations they have under the UN Charter. At the same time, however, the Charter prohibits a decision-making role for nongovernmental organizations. This has not, however, diminished their desire to participate, nor has it negated the crucial contributions they can make. One key role they have played is to push national governments to become more involved in environmental treaty making. Ultimately, nongovernmental organizations are the linchpin between domestic politics and global treaty making.

## Why Countries Participate

There are several types of benefits that countries can realize from active involvement in global environmental treaty making. The first is being able to shape international policy so that it responds to domestic priorities. Countries that are "out of the loop" are not as likely to find their needs well met by the treaties that emerge. A second benefit of participation is the chance to set a precedent or strike a deal that will be helpful later on. This can be accomplished by responding to requests for support from allies, or offering to join a winning coalition in exchange for help in the future. Because the size and solidarity of winning coalitions make a difference, countries are often wooed by allies who need their votes and are willing to promise assistance or support in the future. There is, of course, another type of benefit: national leaders can increase their domestic popularity by demonstrating leadership on the world stage. Even a failed effort to win international support for a proposed global treaty-making effort can redound to a national leader's political benefit at home. Finally, recent global environmental treaties have offered financial compensation to developing countries. Because these funds can be used to underwrite important domestic projects, they may help to bring some countries that otherwise would have remained uninvolved into environmental treaty negotiations.

There are also defensive reasons to participate in treaty making, including the possibility of avoiding costs and protecting national interests. An individual nation may choose to "sit out" or ignore a treaty-making effort entirely, but there is a possibility that a treaty signed by others may at some point constitute new international laws that will apply to all countries, whether or not they were signatories. Thus, from the standpoint of a national leader, it may be better to participate, get credit "at home" for being involved, while working to fend off pressures to conform to requirements that may eventually be incorporated into international law.

Recent global environmental treaties promise aid to developing countries, implicitly committing developed countries to tax themselves to cover the cost of this assistance. Countries worried about increasing pressure to offer greater amounts of official development aid (ODA) realize that higher targets for ODA could be set in the course of environmental treaty negotiation obliging them to increase the assistance they currently provide. So, the financial risks of remaining on the sidelines while new standards of development assistance are set, could be high. (It is worth nothing, in this context, that the $125 billion in aid cited at the Earth Summit as the amount that would be needed to implement Agenda 21 would more than double the $54 billion that the individual nations provided in 1990 for bilateral and multilateral development assistance.)

It may make sense for a country to participate in a treaty negotiation even if that country has no intention of signing the treaty under discussion. Because countries are not legally obliged to sign a treaty even if they participated actively in drafting it, they might attempt to influence the content of an accord and then refuse to sign. As Appendix A indicates, most treaties prior to the Earth Summit were signed by relatively few countries. For example, only fifty-four countries were contracting parties to the Vienna Convention on Substances that Deplete the Ozone Layer, signed initially in 1985. Just forty-nine countries signed the RAMSAR treaty on wetlands in 1971. Only fifty-one countries have ratified the MARPOL ship pollution treaty, signed in 1978. More than a third of the countries in Africa have ratified fewer than half the sixteen treaties listed in Appendix A. More than half the countries in Africa and Asia have never ratified the London Dumping Convention, approved the Montreal Protocol, or supported the Basel Convention on the Transboundary Movements of Hazardous Wastes and their Disposal.

The number of countries signing environmental treaties in the past was surprisingly small, yet I suspect that the increasingly larger numbers of countries now signing environmental accords, a phenomenon that began at the Rio Earth Summit, will continue. There are growing pressures, both at the international and domestic levels, for nations to sign new environmental treaties. Such pressures are the product of intense public campaigns by nongovernmental groups, international environmental organizations, multilateral lending agencies, and even national business organizations that find global "harmonization" of environmental regulations advantageous. This is also likely to correlate with growing domestic pressure from nongovernmental organizations (NGOs) and demands from international institutions and international nongovernmental organizations to be able to participate more directly in the treaty-making process.

It is relatively easy for a country to gain the benefits of global environmental treaties without signing them, but only if enough other countries sign so that the treaty becomes official. The United States played a role in the 1992 Biodiversity Convention negotiations even though it did not sign at Rio, that is, U.S. negotiators influenced both the substance and scope of the treaty, despite the fact that the United States refused to sign. Thus, countries that are signatories will adopt many of the provisions of the treaty that the United States was eager to have included, even though the

United States was not (until President Clinton changed course) a signatory. American corporations and citizens would not have been bound by law to live with provisions of a treaty that their government found unacceptable.

The United States also refused to ratify the Law of the Sea Treaty. It has never ratified the Basel Convention, and, as mentioned above, President Bush refused to sign the Biodiversity Convention at the Earth Summit. Obviously, the U.S. leadership believes that its interests are not well served by these treaties. Having participated in the negotiations, and in some cases—like the Law of the Sea negotiations—played a major role in shaping the content of the agreement, the United States nevertheless failed to ratify. Because its unwillingness to sign did not stall action entirely, the United States could not be blamed for halting an important worldwide effort. The elements of the Law of the Sea Treaty of which it did approve are now part of the body of common law that the United States accepts (and, indeed, takes advantage of); the aspects it did not like, it can ignore with impunity.[1]

The benefits of participating in treaty drafting are substantial and the costs or risks are low. The short-term political benefits—domestic, international, or personal—can be realized whether or not a country ultimately chooses to sign or ratify. As long as national governments have complete control over the treaty-making process, the benefits of participating in treaty drafting will be high and the costs of failing to sign will be low. If nongovernmental interests were to play a larger role in the entire process of treaty drafting, however, it would be more difficult for official national representatives to reap short-term political benefits while ignoring the long-term environmental costs of weak treaties or inaction. If nongovernmental interests had a formal role in the adoption of treaties, the chances that countries would participate but not sign would be reduced because the NGOs involved would probably have more clout and credibility in domestic debates and probably bring increased pressure on national leaders to sign. This may be why the United Nations is reluctant to redefine the role of unofficials in the organization's activities.

## Only Countries Vote

One model for the NGO participation evolves from the May 1990 regional preparatory conference of the Economic Commission for Europe, held in Bergen, Norway. Organizers of the Bergen session took unprecedented steps to ensure NGO participation. NGOs were represented by 173 delegates from five designated sectors (youth, trade unions, industry, science, and voluntary organizations). The conference was divided into two parts: a working session, followed by a ministerial session, during which final negotiations took place. During the working session, NGO representatives were full partners with national delegates, serving as vice presidents in the sessions and preparing working papers. The working session concluded with adoption of a "Joint Agenda for Action" prepared with the full cooperation of NGO and government delegates. Although NGOs had only observer status during the ministerial session, they were allowed to address the session and were included as official delegates from ten of the thirty-four member states. At the conclusion of the Bergen conference, the commission recommended that nongovernmental organizations be allowed to participate fully in the work of other regional commissions of the United Nations and in the Earth Summit preparatory meetings.

At the second PrepCom meeting, UNCED Secretary-General Maurice Strong enthusiastically embraced the Bergen model. Strong observed that the community of NGOs could "enrich and enhance the deliberations of the conference and its preparatory process." It could also "serve as an important channel for the dissemination of conference results and mobilize public support for strengthened environmental policies at the national and international levels." Strong's report included a recommendation that NGOs be actively involved at the national and regional levels, along the lines of the Bergen experience, and contribute actively during all UNCED working sessions (Lindborg, 1992:14).

Strong's recommendations were opposed by representatives of Mauritania and Tunisia, and ultimately defeated. It was agreed, instead, that nongovernmental organizations would have no negotiating role in the work of the PrepCom. Moreover, they would be permitted only to "make written presentations in the preparatory process through the Secretariat." Their statements would "not be issued as official documents." NGOs that had not been granted official consultative status by the UN Economic and Social Council would be allowed only to ask to speak briefly at meetings. If the number of such requests grew too large, the PrepCom would request that NGOs form themselves into constituencies and each constituency would be required to designate a speaker (Lindborg, 1992:14).

The majority of recent treaty-making conferences have extended some version of observer status to NGOs. Observers have a variety of privileges, including the ability to submit papers and documents into the record, permission to address various sessions, or attendance at sessions as nonvoting participants. It is important, however, that final negotiations usually occur either in closed plenary sessions or, if NGOs are present, in closed informal meetings. For example, NGOs were a major factor in mobilizing public opinion during the ozone negotiations, but they were barred from some of the executive committee meetings. Similarly, the Basel Convention did not allow NGOs to participate in working groups, although they were permitted to attend plenary sessions. NGOs played a more substantial role in the CITES treaty negotiations: any qualified NGO could participate on a nonvoting basis, unless at least one-third of the parties objected. They were given numerous opportunities to speak during both committee meetings and plenary sessions.

As this summary suggests, only countries have official voting power within the UN treaty-making system, but on an ad hoc basis, NGOs have been given substantial roles—up to and including shared responsibility for managing working sessions, and speaking (although not voting) at formal plenary meetings at which final decisions are made. The rights accorded to NGOs, however, are unpredictable.

## The Majority Does Not Rule

There is no requirement in the Vienna Convention on the Law of Treaties that a minimum number of countries participate in any global environmental treaty-making effort. That is, a handful of countries can decide to organize a conference, prepare a convention, adopt protocols, and implement monitoring and enforcement procedures if they choose to. Indeed, there are many bilateral and regional environmental agreements that concern (and bind) only a few signatories. What is confusing is the relationship between treaties of this sort, national sovereignty, and the scope of international law.

Under the United Nations Charter, nations are guaranteed sovereignty. This means that they must consent to be bound by each treaty. Typically, consent is expressed not just by a head of state's signing and a legislative body's ratifying an accord but by the enactment of civil laws requiring citizens and officials of a ratifying country to comply with the terms of a treaty.

Countries that do not give their consent, however, are still part of the international "system." Even if they fail to ratify a treaty that comes into force or refuse to enact parallel domestic legislation, that country and its citizens and corporations may find themselves compelled to abide by "customary law" (mentioned in Chapter 2 and discussed further in Chapter 6).

Thus, countries and citizens in countries that are not signatories to a treaty may face obligations nevertheless. These can come into play when other countries refer to a treaty as the source of standards in bilateral relations. They can also come into play when domestic or international courts are asked to hear cases that involve international interactions. In short, it does not take a majority of UN members as signatories of a global treaty to establish international standards or norms. Although countries are sovereign, and may not give their consent to a particular treaty, they are part of an intergovernmental system that expects them to meet common standards of behavior. A failure to behave as expected may not lead to punishment (see Chapter 6 for a fuller discussion of treaty enforcement), but it may lead to other costly and politically damaging outcomes, the most injurious of which is political embarrassment at home.

The United Nations operates in a fashion that does not give the majority of countries any assurance of having their way, especially if they refuse to participate in treaty making. Nor does it guarantee a minority—that chooses not to participate—that its interests will be protected. There are no requirements that a minimum number of countries support a treaty before it can come into force. There is no requirement for regional representation either during treaty drafting or at the point of ratification. Whole sections of the world may object to treaties that nevertheless come into force, as was the case, for example, when most African nations refused to sign the Basel Convention. There is not even any formal requirement that a fixed percentage of countries that ratify a treaty must vote to amend it. This, too, is handled on an ad hoc basis; the decision is made by the signatories themselves at the point at which they sign a convention.

## "Unofficials" Have Key Roles to Play

In such an open-ended system, with no central authority to call UN members to account or to ensure their participation in global environmental treaty making, it falls to "unofficials," particularly nongovernmental organizations within each country, to hold their governments accountable. "Unofficials" have several crucial roles to play in the process. They can serve as scientific advisers or information gatherers at the point at which risks are being defined or problems are being diagnosed. They can play the role of advocates, mobilizing public opinion within each country as well as on a worldwide basis, pressing heads of state to advance an issue higher up the political agenda.

Unofficials can also make negotiations more democratic, ensuring that the concerns of segments of the population that may not be important to certain national leaders are nevertheless addressed by international assemblies. They may also assume the role of change agent, promoting new and different policy approaches that have not yet won support in international bureaucratic ranks. Unofficials, in addition, can serve as monitors, providing a key independent check on the information provided by official sources, or gathering data when countries fail to meet their reporting requirements. Finally, unofficials can serve as intermediaries or facilitators, suggesting and helping to implement action on stop-gap measures when treaties do not produce results or there is no time to move collectively when formal treaties have clearly failed.

Another way of classifying the roles that unofficials play in global environmental treaty making is to distinguish between "internal" and "external" modes of participation. Internal functions include putting pressure on a country to participate in a treaty-making effort, and working to influence the position a country takes during treaty negotiations by forging domestic coalitions and mobilizing public opinion. For example, unofficials can put public pressure on a country to sign a treaty even when the domestic leadership prefers to hold out for something more. They can also serve as a watchdog agency, forcing a country to meet the provisions of treaties it has signed, particularly by using domestic courts to challenge governments, companies, and others if they are not complying. Even if national leaders are free to ignore the jurisdiction of the World Court, nongovernmental organizations can sometimes use national courts to constrain governmental leaders, corporations, and individual citizens in ways that are enforceable.

External functions are generally handled by nongovernmental interests that cross political boundaries, particularly international business organizations, scientific associations, voluntary organizations, religious groups, and associations of grass-roots groups. These functions include urging the United Nations to add an environmental issue to its agenda, and gathering evidence to help frame or define a problem or a threat in ways that influence the work of official UN-sanctioned conferences. Unofficials, particularly independent researchers and scholars, can help to develop the theoretical justification for a particular response or "solution"; they can help to build "winning" coalitions among countries that may not have significant bilateral dealings with each other, or even have other reasons not to collaborate. Finally, unofficials can help to implement the terms of treaties by volunteering to assist countries that do not have the necessary expertise to meet their obligations.

Given this multiplicity of roles and functions, it is not surprising that unofficials want more recognition—indeed, a guarantee—that their involvement will not be blocked by the United Nations and its member institutions. Nongovernmental interests want the United Nations to acknowledge formally their right to participate. At present, at the outset of each treaty-making effort, unofficials must invest substantial organizational resources in pleading for the right to be at the negotiation table. Often, as was the case at the Rio Earth Summit, they are forced to settle for parallel conferences or restricted observer status. These alternatives may lead over time to changes in the views of members of formal national delegations, but often they do not. The parallel conference format that was so potent at Stockholm—from which messages and ideas were carried back to the formal sessions by key members of national delegations—was not nearly as effective at the Earth Summit. The "Rio Global Forum," as it was called, produced more than three dozen parallel treaties but failed to have the impact on the work of the formal national decision makers that unofficials had hoped it would.

Unofficials have played a role in the process for several decades and, in some instances (such as the CITES agreement), shoulder major responsibility for treaty implementation. Basking in the success of their substantial role at Bergen, unofficials are pushing hard for a guarantee of direct involvement in all treaty making, without the need to plead their case each time a new treaty-making effort gets under way. The Rio PrepCom meetings underscore the significance of these concerns. Much of the PrepComs' time was spent redebating what the role of unofficials would be. Each time a treaty-making effort gets under way, unofficials face substantial resistance to their participation. They want to institutionalize something closer to a full-fledged partnership with the governmental members of the United Nations.

The exact form that partnership should take is not clear, but several principles that might guide its design are. First, the various segments of the unofficial community should be recognized as separate and distinct. At the second PrepCom in August 1990, in Nairobi, the Environmental Liaison Center International, an umbrella NGO headquartered in Africa, issued a statement indicating that "NGOs are nonprofit, non-party political organizations, including groupings such as environment and development, youth, indigenous people, consumer, and religious. Organizations of industry, trade unions, parliamentarians, academics, and local authorities are not NGOs." They are, however, unofficials. The International Facilitating Committee—created by the Geneva-based Center for Our Common Future, and charged with managing the parallel NGO conference in Rio—took a more inclusive approach. It used the all-embracing term *independent sector,* and identified eleven independent subsectors: business and industry, indigenous peoples, youth, students, scientific organizations, women, trade unions, religious/interfaith groups, the media, grass-roots farmers and peasants, and human rights/peace organizations.[2]

Within the community of nongovernmental interest groups (or NGIs, as I call them), there is much debate on the inclusion of business. The International Facilitating Committee urges that business interests be given a place at the table; the Environmental Liaison Center International does not. In part, this reflects a perception that when business representatives participate as nongovernmental interests, they skew the discussion toward economic self-interest and impede progress toward a broader conception of natural resources as "the heritage of mankind." This perception is underscored by recent charges by the nonprofit sector that some business interests are creating nonprofit NGOs as "fronts" (such as the National Wetlands Coalition sponsored by the oil industries) to pursue a business agenda.[3]

Multiple subsectors of the independent sector must be included. Each subsector needs to be able to caucus and choose its own representatives to participate in each treaty-making effort. Business, as well as all the other subsectors, ought to be included to ensure that exclusivity is not used as an argument against the legitimate demand of the NGIs to be given a place in the negotiation process.

A second principle that should guide the design of a new partnership between the United Nations and NGIs is that nongovernmental interests need to be "at the table" at all stages of the treaty-making process. Although unofficials cannot be given voting power within the context of a UN-sponsored arrangement, the goal in treaty making is consensus, anyway, rather than majority rule. Thus, who has and does not have voting power is not necessarily a significant issue.

In any consensus-seeking context, along with the right to be heard comes the responsibility for taking account of the concerns of others. Hence, groups that are not prepared to accept responsibility for working toward an informed consensus should be denied an invitation to participate in further treaty-making negotiations. Guerrilla tactics ought not be a reason to exclude groups from the dialogue, but at some point, when the vast majority of NGIs finds that it cannot conduct its internal negotiations or constructive exchanges with official delegates, disruptive groups must be forced to leave. It is up to the NGIs to police themselves, or they will lose their place "at the table" with official delegates.

The goal in all treaty-making negotiations ought to be to seek consensus, but this does not necessarily mean that an effort has failed if unanimity is not achieved. Instead, the burden should be on the convener or secretariat for each treaty negotiation, who must decide when an effort to seek consensus has gone as far as it possibly can. At that point, a decision (in the form of an agreement to sign) must be made by each stakeholder. In the UN context, only countries vote, but each country's vote is influenced by domestic political considerations that are, in turn, shaped by the position that domestic and international NGIs have taken.

Despite all the important functions that nongovernmental interests can add to in the treaty-making process, there is still value in their remaining distinct from governmental interests. Some nongovernmental interests serve as members of national delegations; others should be present as independent actors, even if somewhat similar interests are represented on both national delegations and at-large NGI associations. Because only countries vote, there need be no fear that nongovernmental interests will be given undue advantage if they are represented in several different ways.

The final principle to guide the design of a new partnership between governments and nongovernmental interests should be an emphasis on informality. Too much of the dialogue at UN-sponsored conferences has become stilted, leading to half-hearted initiatives that value caution far more than imagination. Even though the language of diplomacy and the rules of official etiquette will, in all likelihood, be preserved indefinitely, more informal give-and-take during working sessions and other portions of official conferences should be encouraged. All parties need to be able to speak freely—to invent without committing—if they are going to engage in fruitful problem solving.

These principles are not overly constraining; they leave room for the exact form of partnership between NGIs and governments to evolve. Moreover, one form of partnership may not be appropriate in all treaty-making situations. Different models may evolve as NGIs demonstrate a clear commitment to responsible and serious participation under various new arrangements. At this point in the evolution of environmental treaty-making efforts, however, one thing is clear: retaining the status quo re-garding the role of nongovernmental interests is unacceptable. They have too much to offer, and they have the potential to fill in the gaps in what governments alone have been able to do. One such area is in representing the interests of future generations.

## Who Represents Future Generations?

Edith Weiss Brown, in her pivotal book, *In Fairness to Future Generations: International Law, Common Patrimony, and Intergenerational Equity* (1989), points out that "many of our actions impose serious environmental bur-dens on future generations." She is concerned, in particular, about "deple-tion of resources, degradation of environmental quality, and discrimina-tory access to the environmental resources and benefits enjoyed by previous generations."

Her goal is to sort out the moral and legal obligations of the current generation to future generations. She begins with the assumption that "humans as a species hold the natural and cultural environment of Earth in common both with other members of the present generation and with other generations, past and future," and asserts that "each generation is both a trustee or custodian of the planet for future generations and a beneficiary of previous generations' stewardship."

In trying to formulate principles to guide human interaction toward intergenerational equity, Brown underscores three considerations: (1) we should encourage equality among generations, neither authorizing the present generation to exploit resources to the exclusion of future generations nor imposing unreasonable burdens on the present generation to meet indeterminate future needs; (2) we should not require one generation to predict the preferences of future generations but, instead, should give future generations flexibility to achieve their goals according to their own values; and (3) we must take account of different cultural traditions and find principles that are attractive to all.

From these considerations she derives three principles:

- Each generation should conserve the diversity of the natural and cultural resource base so that it does not unduly restrict the options available to future generations in solving their problems and satisfying their own values, and each generation is entitled to a diversity comparable to that of previous generations. This principle she calls the conservation of options.
- Each generation should maintain the quality of the planet so that it is passed on in no worse condition than the generation received it, and each generation is entitled to an environmental quality comparable to that enjoyed by previous generations. This principle she calls the conservation of equality.
- Each generation should provide its members with equitable rights of access to the planetary legacy of past generations and should conserve this access for future generations. This principle she calls the conservation of access.

Brown is then faced with the difficult task of figuring out how these objectives might be met. Taking a legal tack, she argues that the principles of intergenerational equity ought to be cast as a set of intergenerational rights and obligations. She and other legal scholars believe that intergenerational rights should probably be added to existing international human rights. She points out that under traditional approaches to the law, rights attach only to identifiable individuals, yet by definition there are no identifiable individuals in future generations because they have yet to be born. The rights of future generations are not individual rights but, rather, rights held by each generation as a class.

So, how best to protect these rights? She suggests that surrogates of future generations might have a part to play. In her view, national governments representing future generations (on a worldwide basis) might play this role. She evolves a legal justification for this approach that I do not find credible. She is more convincing when she speaks of nongovernmental interests or specially appointed ombudsmen being tapped to perform as advocates for future generations. In the same way that U.S. courts often appoint a guardian *ad litem* to represent the interests of children in divorce actions (or that localities or nongovernmental interests can represent future generations in Superfund cleanup decision making), Brown believes that individuals or NGIs could be selected to speak for future generations.

Assume, for the sake of argument, that such individuals or groups could be found. Would they be taken seriously? In Brown's model, the interests of future generations would be argued before the World Court. To the extent that a statement of "Planetary Obligations and Rights" (of the sort described in Appendix B) were adopted by the United Nations, the World Court might well adjudicate claims that the rights of future generations were being abridged by the actions of the current generation. And, claims of this sort could reasonably be argued by nongovernmental representatives of future generations. As long as there is a judge to adjudicate the claims, and a clear statement of the law specifying the rights of future generations and the obligations of the current generation, her idea might work.

How, though, can the interests of future generations be represented in treaty negotiations, where there is no judge to weigh the evidence and impose a decision? What clout would the same surrogates have in global environmental treaty-making negotiations, where the dominant decision-making criterion is not the "rule of law" but, rather, political give-and-take informed by scientific advice? Without a judge and a clear statement of rights and obligations that must be respected, the notion of a guardian *ad litem* representing future generations falls apart.

In a bargaining process, part of the credibility and clout that a negotiator brings to the table is the ability to commit his or her constituents to a future course of action. Even if representatives of future generations could be found, they would have no way of making credible commitments on behalf of their constituents. Moreover, they could not speak credibly about their "clients'" needs, priorities, or attitudes toward possible trade-offs. Without the equivalent of a judge to enforce the recommendations of the guardian *ad litem*, the spokesperson for future generations can do little more than raise ethical or moral concerns. As important as these may be, it is difficult to imagine that they would be sufficient to induce national leaders to accept short-term "losses" in exchange for long-term environmental gains for future generations. Surrogates of future generations could bring the force of moral arguments to bear—and NGIs could do this much more effectively than a particular world leader—but I doubt they would have a substantial impact on the substance of most treaty negotiations.

If we cannot protect the interests of future generations by relying on NGIs to represent their interests in treaty negotiations, how ought these interests to be taken into account? Brown introduces several other ideas, including intergenerational conservation assessments that force the present generation to compensate future generations for adverse impacts caused by present action, a greater commitment to scientific and technological research to assess risks, increases in the efficiency of the extraction and use of resources, development of substitutes (prior to the utilization of all remaining nonrenewables); education to foster a new planetary ethos rooted in a sense of belonging to a community of past, present, and future generations; and intergenerational trust funds financed by a global user's fee or toll (such as a carbon tax), which could be seen as the price each generation must pay for using the planet and to fulfill its obligation to future generations.

These ideas may have some promise, but I am not optimistic, especially in a time of worldwide recession, about strategies that rely on taxing current users for the cost of the impacts they are creating for future generations. Unfortunately, future generations do not vote in the present. Moreover, like most market-oriented approaches (e.g., trying to ensure that the true costs of environmental damage are reflected in the current price of goods and services), these strategies minimize the significance of ecosystem maintenance, biodiversity, and the social importance of certain resource-utilization patterns that are impossible to price in current dollars.

The most plausible strategy for protecting the interests of future generations is to insist on the imposition of a sustainable development rule in all global environmental decision making as well as at the national level. NGIs have a major role to play in ensuring that the goal of sustainability is pursued actively by governments and multilateral agencies. If the multilateral lending institutions insist that only "sustainable" projects shall receive funding, there is a reasonable chance that the interests of future generations will indeed be served.

As Brown points out, this was the key recommendation of the Brundtland Report. Yet, sustainable use of renewable resources (linked with monitoring of the diversity and quality of the environment) are still elusive goals, in part because they are difficult (both technically and politically) to spell out in detail. One of the most helpful discussions of what sustainability entails is provided by Herman Daly in *Steady State Economics*. Daly (1992:241–256) writes: "Under ideal conditions the market can find an optimal allocation of resources, but the market cannot find an optimal scale any more than it can find an optimal distribution of resources. This requires the application of ethical and ecological considerations."

Daly also explains that much of the confusion about sustainability can be traced to the confusion between *growth* and *development*. *Growth*, Daly suggests, should be used to refer to the quantitative scale of the physical dimensions of the economy. *Development*, on the other hand, should refer to "qualitative improvement." Daly advocates "a steady-state economy that develops without growing, just as the planet earth develops without growing." Limits to growth, therefore, "do not imply limits to development."

The ideology of growth has been seductive because it seems to offer a potential solution to poverty without requiring, as Daly points out, "the moral discipline of sharing" or population control. The opponents of efforts to limit growth wrongly assume that diminishing levels of growth "will make us poorer rather than richer." Thus, confusing growth with development is not only incorrect but fails to take account of the costs of unsustainable growth patterns.

As Daly and others have noted, the present system of national accounts treats receipts from the sale of natural assets as income, thus giving countries the illusion that they are better off than they are. These should actually be tallied as depreciated investments. The regeneration of natural capital has, for too long, been perceived as unimportant because it has not been a limiting factor. Now, however, we are entering an era in which our remaining natural assets will be a limiting factor. Second, neoclassical economics has taught that manufactured capital is a near-perfect substitute for natural resources and, consequently, for the stock of natural capital that yields the flow of these natural resources. Daly points out that contrary to neoclassical assumptions, natural and manufactured capital are more complements than substitutes, with natural capital increasingly replacing manufactured products as the limiting factor in development. An operational approach to ensuring sustainability, therefore, that does not hinge on the availability of substitutes is to adjust the system of national accounts. As Daly suggests, this should include subtracting an estimate of the depreciated value of natural capital from our estimated resources. We should also subtract an estimate of the expenditures necessary to protect ourselves against the unwanted side effects of production.

For the Brundtland Commission's ideas to work in practice, the "basic needs of the present generation" must be distinguished from extravagant wants. Second, our estimates of future generations' abilities to meet their own needs should be based on realistic estimate of the likelihood that we will be able to substitute capital for natural resources in the future. We ought to be reasonably conservative in making this estimate.

The most obvious approach to sustainable development is to ensure that renewable resources are exploited on a sustainable-yield basis. Determining such levels, however, is not entirely straightforward. Sustainable yield can be defined in terms of profit maximization or biological sustainability. It is even more difficult to figure out the "sustainable use" of nonrenewable resources. One technique is to calculate the rate of use at which price is equal to that of its nearest renewable substitute. In other words, nonrenewable resources should be priced according to their long-run replacement cost. Accounting techniques are available that do this without requiring the identification of a specific long-term renewable substitute.[4]

If we take sustainability as our guiding principle, then all development projects should, ideally, be sustainable. Whenever that is not possible, as with nonrenewable resource extraction, Daly and others suggest pairing unsustainable projects with complementary projects that insure sustainability for the two taken together. Also, if development activities must be sustainable, then it is inappropriate to calculate the benefits of a sustainable project or policy alternative by comparing it with an unsustainable option, that is by using a discount rate that reflects rates of return on alternative uses of capital that are themselves unsustainable.

Sustainability of a development project is a benefit. In general, an extra benefit usually requires an extra cost. A policy of sustainability means that we are willing to pay that extra cost, at least within reason. NGIs are more likely than governments to advocate the appropriateness of this trade-off. They also represent the constituency that must bear this cost. National leaders, on the other hand, because of their shorter time horizon and accountability to only the current generation of voters, will not be as effective in promoting these trade-offs. To the extent the United Nations expects to implement Agenda 21 and its long-term commitment to sustainable development, it will need to give NGIs more responsibility for making the necessary trade-offs.

## The Power of the Secretariat

The way that a secretariat for a treaty negotiation handles competing interests, including the tension between the interests of the current generation and future generations, is critical to the UN's effort to promote sustainable development. Traditionally, secretariats have played relatively passive roles. At the extreme, they have been unwilling to take the initiative, offering advice only when it is requested (and then never publicly), keeping to a conservative interpretation of the mandate of the group, and never doing anything to annoy the parties. Although recent UN secretaries-general have broken out of this mold, firmly establishing the legitimacy, authority, and acceptability of the UN executive as an impartial intervenor in international conflicts, secretariats for global environmental treaty making have not yet achieved an activist status of this sort.

The traditional model of the secretariat is especially inadequate when it comes to international environmental negotiations. It reflects an era when only clearly identifiable nation-states—represented solely by their elected leaders—were stakeholders in international negotiations. This is obviously not the case with environmental issues, where stakeholders include the broad range of nongovernmental interests described above.

To deal effectively with the complexities and uncertainties associated with environmental negotiations, secretariats must have a clear mandate to be more activist and creative, particularly in their functions as facilitators and mediators (Sandford, 1992). Secretariats are often underutilized in this regard. They have the potential to play a significant and positive role in environmental conflict management and dispute resolution.

The core structure and function of a secretariat can remain essentially the same while facilitation responsibilities are added. To enhance the perceived neutrality of the secretariat, it may be helpful to rotate the assignment of responsibility for secretarial duties. Diversity of the secretariat staff can also help to ensure that all participating countries and NGIs can find someone in the secretariat with whom they can comfortably speak. At least partial funding from the regular UN budget is required to support all secretariats; otherwise they will be perceived as narrowly beholden to the parties to treaties who are paying the bills. Secretariat functions need to emphasize multiple roles at each of the three basic stages of the treaty-making process: prenegotiation, negotiation, and implementation. The secretariat needs to play an active role in bringing all stakeholding parties—particularly NGIs—to the negotiating table, facilitating collaborative research or what is called joint fact-finding, and helping the parties formulate ground rules to guide their negotiations.

During the formal give-and-take of bargaining, the secretariat should not be afraid to "float" specific proposals or to formulate packages that might bridge points of disagreement. The secretariat should be the primary point of contact for nongovernmental interests that find national leaders unwilling to listen to their ideas. Sometimes nongovernmental interests may be better off channeling their ideas through the secretariat and having draft proposals come directly from the secretariat to the national governments involved.

During the postnegotiation stage, the secretariat should be the party responsible for collecting required reports, organizing follow-up sessions to review scientific evidence, and, perhaps, for mediating any disputes concerning compliance. Again, NGIs may be better off raising a concern with the secretariat and letting the staff pursue the initial investigation. If they are not satisfied, of course, NGIs can pursue concerns about compliance on their own. These suggestions represent no diminution in the

Table 3   Functions of an Environmental Secretariat

| Stages in Treaty Making | Secretariat Function |
|---|---|
| Prenegotiation | |
| | Anticipates and diagnoses conflicts |
| | Initiates consultations among members and relevant stakeholders |
| | Initiates stakeholder identification; actively seeks out representatives and potential stakeholders |
| | Facilitates negotiation and dispute-resolution training for members, stakeholders, and secretariat staff |
| | Facilitates problem-solving workshops |
| | Facilitates collaborative fact-finding efforts |
| | Acts as intervenor as required |
| Negotiation | |
| Option generation | Acts as intervenor as required |
| | Facilitates use of option-generation processes with members and stakeholders regarding issue-linkage, incentives/compensation/compliance |
| Package agreement | Prepares option packages in consultation with members and stakeholders |
| Draft treaty | Facilitates development of single negotiating text |
| | Ensures inclusion of conflict management and dispute resolution provisions |
| Signing of treaty | Shuttle consultation |
| Ratification | Shuttle consultation and/or intervention |
| | Management assistance to deal with issues arising during this period |
| Implementation | |
| Monitoring | Designated body responsible for monitoring agreement(s) according to objective/predetermined criteria developed during earlier stages |
| Compliance | Oversees compliance monitoring |
| | Reports violations to full group |
| | Implements agreed procedure to deal with violations |
| Renegotiation | First point of contact if renegotiation needed |

*Source:* Rosemary Sandford, "Secretariats and International Environmental Negotiations," in *International Environmental Treatymaking,* ed. Lawrence E. Susskind, Eric Jay Dolin, and J. William Breslin (Cambridge, Mass.: Program on Negotiation at Harvard Law School), 1992.

decision-making powers of the parties, nor do they require a large permanent bureaucracy. Secretariat teams can be appointed for each treaty-making effort. These responsibilities can and should rotate from group to group and location to location.

Table 3 indicates the range of roles that an activist secretariat can play at each stage in the treaty-making process. If nongovernmental interests are going to have a greater role in the UN system, it will fall to the secretariats to handle the additional management responsibilities.

## There Is No Consensus-Building Process

Global environmental treaty making and the international cooperation needed to implement effective treaties require extensive consensus building, which, in turn, requires effective ad hoc representation of all the stakeholders, face-to-face interaction among skilled representatives of the stakeholding interests, a real give-and-take aimed at maximizing joint gains, facilitation by appropriate neutral parties at various points in the process, informality that allows the parties to speak their minds, and extensive prenegotiation that ensures opportunities for joint problem solving. At the present time, the basic structure of the United Nations—with its limited emphasis on national representation and the maintenance of sovereignty—works against these prerequisites.

The best way of countering this, without dismantling the structure of the UN system, is to guarantee representatives of nongovernmental interests a larger role as long as they live by rules and accept responsibilities spelled out ahead of time. A new partnership between government and NGIs should be based on the four principles enumerated earlier: all segments of the NGI community should be invited to participate, including business; NGIs should be involved at the table in all stages of treaty negotiation; NGIs should not be given voting power (unless they are part of national delegations), but consensus and not majority rule should be the decision-making mode; and all interactions should stress informal problem solving to the greatest extent possible.

Such partnerships need to be assisted by activist secretariats (which may draw on the services of external neutrals, including skilled mediators). NGIs need to adhere to the ground rules that are jointly devised regarding their participation in treaty negotiations. The key is to rely on unofficials to play the various roles they are best suited to play. The UN system, relying as it does on states, cannot achieve its objective of sustainable development and meet its obligations to future generations unless NGIs or unofficials are given a more explicit set of responsibilities than they have at present.

# CHAPTER 4

# The Need for a Better Balance Between Science and Politics

Independent scientific investigations play a role in environmental treaty making, but they are intertwined with, not separate from, political considerations. Gareth Porter and Janet Brown, in their excellent textbook, *Global Environmental Politics*, suggest that global environmental negotiations involve four political processes, "issue definition, factfinding, bargaining, and regime strengthening." Scientific investigations have been an integral part of each of these four processes, although when and how they are used could certainly be improved.

Porter and Brown suggest that the process of issue definition brings problems to the attention of the international community and "identifies the scope and magnitude of the environmental threat, its primary causes, and the type of international action" required to address it. Scientific evidence should be prominent at this early stage in negotiations as governmental and nongovernmental actors attempt to justify their claims about the threats involved. Once issues are identified, fact-finding should bring "parties together in an attempt to establish a baseline of facts on which there is agreement and to clarify the scope and nature of differences in the understanding of the problem and possible policy options for international action." When there is no joint fact-finding, Porter and Brown suggest, scientific information is often challenged by states that have their own reasons for opposing international action. This brings competing experts into conflict with each other, triggers a problematic deterioration in the level of trust among the stakeholders, and undermines the public's willingness to give significant weight to scientific considerations.

Porter and Brown also suggest that, in most cases, fact-finding quickly becomes indistinguishable from bargaining. Bargaining hinges on the leverage and cohesion of veto coalitions, groups of states that can block international cooperation.[1] When a negotiated agreement is reached, it is usually because key members of a veto coalition defected or conceded a major point. Although scientific revelations can sometimes accelerate or facilitate such defections or concessions, they usually occur because one party or coalition reduces its political demands. Instead of a binding protocol, for example, proponents may agree to settle for a less demanding framework convention (requiring no specific action, setting no deadlines, or offering fewer resources) in order to get a blocking coalition to concede. Toward the end of the bargaining process, scientific evidence becomes less and less important, while political give-and-take dominates.

Regime strengthening, the final process that Porter and Brown describe, occurs after a first round of agreement has been reached. It should reflect an improved understanding of the environmental problem. Thus, scientific evidence, especially the product of joint monitoring or collaborative research, should be given substantial weight. Most treaty modifications involving adoption of subsequent protocols or amendments, however, are as likely to be a response to domestic political forces as they are to increased scientific understanding.

A review of most of the international treaties negotiated since the 1972 Stockholm conference shows that scientific evidence has played a surprisingly small role in issue definition, fact-finding, bargaining, and regime strengthening.[2] Porter and Brown report that scientific evidence did help to "galvanize international action" (that is, define issues and propel bargaining) on acid rain and ozone depletion but was secondary or irrelevant in shaping the terms of the treaties dealing with whaling, hazardous waste trade, tropical deforestation, Antarctic mineral exploration, and trade in African elephant ivory. I would expand their first list (where science was very important) to include the recent biodiversity negotiations but add to the second list (where it did not play a crucial role) ocean dumping, world heritage, wetlands and migratory species protection, and rewriting the Law of the Sea.

There are several reasons that scientific findings have less impact than many people expect. Key among them is the fact that environmental treaty negotiations deal with incredibly complex, frequently intersecting systems about which there is still only a limited understanding. The best possible analytical efforts, including studies of past patterns of ecological change, models of current human-environment interactions, and forecasts of long-term environmental impacts, produce rough estimates at best. Because they are not definitive, they have less impact than they otherwise might. Second, there will always be self-interested actors willing to exploit scientific uncertainty for their own ends, arguing against any global action (that would hurt them) on the grounds that a fuller understanding is required before a clear course of action can be charted. When scientists acknowledge uncertainty, they allow political actors greater control over decision making. And third, within the scientific community there are experts who relish a confrontation (especially debates that put them at the center of attention); unfortunately, the press and the general public, unable to discern the significance of intramural disagreements among experts, assume that it is unwise or unsafe to move ahead until the "full truth" emerges. The insights that are available are then brushed aside.

Global environmental threats often burst into the public's attention as a result of a highly publicized emergency or disaster. Efforts to put such events in context (for example, to explain a famine in terms of cyclical weather patterns) are viewed as a cover-up in some quarters. Evenhanded scientific inquiries are no match for the public clamor caused by emotional televised accounts of terrible disasters. The chances that a famine or a hot summer are the result of "global warming" are practically nil; however, the media have no qualms about using current events to dramatize the potential effects of climate change. To counteract this kind of distortion, scientists should probably play more of a role in issue definition than they currently do.

Many observers believe that the next step, fact-finding, should presumably be the exclusive domain of scientists. In general, the lay public believes that either there is an environmental problem or there is not, and that knowledgeable experts, sifting through the evidence, should be able to warn or reassure appropriately. This turns out not to be the case. For example, if a resource is disappearing at a startling rate but substitutes are readily available, do we have a problem? If a source of pollution is clear, but the technology exists to blunt the immediate impacts (such as a filter that can be placed at the end of a smokestack), is the pollution a problem that requires closing down a plant? If experiments on rats show that very large doses of a pollutant can be carcinogenic, is that sufficient reason to believe that very small amounts of that substance in the atmosphere are a threat to human health? Although the potential safety risks associated with a large-scale development project are substantial if something goes wrong but the chances of such an accident's occurring are infinitesimal, should the project be canceled? There are numerous nonobjective or nonexpert judgments involved in answering questions like these. Pure or normal science offers no special advantage in addressing them. Because the answers depend more on the questioner's philosophical orientation than on rigorous methods of analysis, reasonably intelligent but untrained individuals can handle them almost as well as experts.

When it comes to bargaining over the actual terms of a treaty, input from scientists is almost always negligible. This is because traditional diplomacy encourages the idea that negotiations ought to reflect politics more than anything else. This emphasis on style over substance has been the source of much of the ineffectiveness of many of the global environmental treaties signed thus far. The details of each treaty, such as which standards must be met by when, are obviously important, but, if these provisions reflect only political horse trading and not a dispassionate appraisal of what will work under different circumstances, the results are likely to be disappointing. Once a problem has been defined, and the scientists have had their say, bargaining tends to be framed mostly in terms of potential economic losses, possible domestic political advantages, and apparent attacks on sovereignty. The likely effectiveness of a treaty in reversing ecological damage, however, is not something that the politicians are capable of deciding alone. Scientists have far too long been the missing link in the bargaining process.

Perhaps in response to the notable unimportance of scientific considerations during the throes of bargaining, scientific investigations have assumed somewhat more importance during postnegotiation assessments of the need for treaty tightening or adjustment. By spelling out explicit monitoring procedures, requiring periodic meetings of the parties to review monitoring data, establishing ongoing joint research activities, and specifying the findings that will, if they are identified, trigger preplanned next steps, the importance of scientific investigation is indeed enhanced. Of course, this is not a guarantee that the parties will actually meet when they are supposed to, or that the monitoring data will be reported reliably, or that the scientific community's subsequent understanding of the problem will be enhanced. Moreover, depending on political pressures at home, elected leaders may try to stonewall the scientific community, regardless of the level of increased understanding.

Over the past several decades, the United States has blocked several environmental-treaty-making efforts by arguing that the scientific evidence did not justify the corrective actions that others were proposing. For example, the United States led the coalition that has made it difficult to produce effective agreements to combat acid rain.[3] It has also argued that too little is known about the problem of global warming to justify the costs of stabilizing greenhouse gas emissions at 1990 levels by the year 2000. When its purposes are served (and we are not alone in this), the United States uses scientific evidence to argue for the actions it favors. When we prefer to take a different political course, we attack the available data as insufficient, regardless of the strength of the worldwide scientific consensus. A telling example of this self-serving philosophy occurred during the

1980s, when the United States initially opposed the rapid phaseout of CFCs. But by the time the Montreal Protocol was negotiated late in the decade, major CFC producers in the United States had developed substitutes that the rest of the world would be able to buy. In a remarkable policy turnaround, the United States agreed that the available evidence required a complete phaseout.

## There Will Always Be Uncertainty

There will always be uncertainty hovering over global environmental treaty negotiations. One way of handling uncertainty is to invest more money in basic environmental research that might produce the scientific equivalent of a "smoking gun." As a result of ongoing British efforts to monitor meteorological change at the South Pole, for example, the hole in the ozone layer was confirmed, and directly linked to CFCs. That "smoking gun" certainly spurred action on the Montreal Protocol—but that was a one-time event. There is no guarantee that expanding basic environmental research will yield the evidence that will reduce uncertainty on other global issues in a timely way. Another strategy would be to organize critical experiments that would establish beyond a doubt that an environmental threat exists, that it is caused in a certain way, and that one and only one response makes sense. The chances are, though, that such experiments will not present themselves.

Nevertheless, the negotiations over mineral exploration in Antarctica and the transboundary shipment of hazardous waste illustrate how bargaining can proceed even when there is great uncertainty about both the scope of the problem or the likely effectiveness of various solutions. Negotiations over an Antarctic mineral regime took place in the absence of any definitive information about the location, extent, or economic value of the mineral resources that might exist. There had been a great deal of speculation based on very limited scientific information and inference, but no hard evidence. Some of the speculation is based on correlations between Antarctica and other mineral-rich continents, but actual geological research on the continent has produced little evidence to support the notion of tremendous riches. This uncertainty, however, provided an incentive to negotiate. The discovery of a valuable resource would only have made the already difficult political problem of how to allocate control over Antarctic resources all the more intractable.

Christopher Beeby has speculated on the problems that would have occurred if a "mountain of gold" had been discovered in New Zealand's Antarctic claim:

> Once the gold was discovered, there would be considerable pressure
> on the New Zealand government to develop rules to regulate its exploita-

tion and to treat the deposit as any other deposit of gold located in New Zealand. This would provoke reaction from nonclaimant countries, rejecting New Zealand's contention that its rules should govern exploitation, which would in turn create the possibility of unregulated development and destabilization of Antarctica similar to that which existed before the Antarctic Treaty and led to its negotiation.[4]

The uncertainty surrounding potential mineral resources in Antarctica seems at first to be different from that surrounding global warming or other large-scale phenomena, because it involves geological factors that are well understood. Yet, the basis for prediction is surprisingly similar: stochastic and probabilistic inference from sparse fieldwork and informed extrapolation. The negotiations revolve around the question of benefit sharing. The parties participate eagerly; more so than they would if only costs were being allocated. Looked at another way, the scientific uncertainty served to increase the value of agreement relative to no agreement. In the Antarctic case, at least, uncertain scientific knowledge made difficult politics a bit easier.

The Antarctic mineral treaty convention is a framework agreement. By adopting it, the parties promised to be bound by the principles, responsibilities, decision-making processes, relationships, and obligations it contains. They did not, however, agree to specific limits, quotas, or conditions because the convention does not contain any. This vagueness may lead to disputes over interpretation of the convention when it is eventually applied.

A tenet of the Basel Convention is that wastes should be disposed of in an environmentally sound manner, defined in Article Two of the convention as requiring "all practicable steps to ensure that hazardous waste or other wastes are managed in a manner which will protect human health and the environment against the adverse effects which may result from such wastes." This language, an attempt to balance the science of hazardous waste management with the politics necessary to achieve agreement on the convention, has come under attack from some environmental NGOs as being too vague. It is not clear whether "environmentally sound" will be determined by the standards of the exporting or the importing country. Because the parties to the treaty are allowed to engage in bilateral agreements resulting in waste trades, it is possible for an importing country to define the term loosely and then sign a long-term import contract. Indeed, there is nothing to stop a developing country from making a bilateral deal with an exporter of waste and then doing what it wants with the waste, even dumping it in the ocean.

The principal debate into which science was injected centered on the question of whether wastes should be disposed of inside generating countries or in the "best" location. One side argued that the present difficulty in siting hazardous waste management facilities in many industrialized countries illustrated how difficult the siting process had become. The general argument advanced by the industrialized countries at Basel was that the best place for hazardous waste disposal should be found, and if that location is abroad, then the wastes should be exported. The developing countries opposed this, pointing to a 1984 UNEP study that revealed that countries lying within or near the tropical zone were, for the most part, poorly suited for hazardous waste disposal because the intense tropical rains they experience could cause landfills to overflow and release their contents.[5] In the end, uncertainty about where the best sites would likely be found, led to a loose framework convention, as well as to a loophole permitting "side deals" between exporters and importers.

Whether or not one supports either treaty, these two examples suggest that negotiations can and will proceed even when there is substantial scientific uncertainty about the scope of the problem or the most desirable solution. They also imply that the greater the degree of uncertainty the more likely the parties are to gravitate toward vague framework conventions. Either the parties to global environmental treaty making can invest in additional scientific research to reduce uncertainty, or they can give science its due and accept the input of independent scientific advisers while acknowledging the inevitable need to balance science and politics.

## Giving Science Its Due

There are still those who would prefer to solve environmental problems by separating scientific analysis from political considerations. Their objective is to isolate, not balance, science and politics. At one point, William Ruckelshaus, then head of the U.S. Environmental Protection Agency, proposed to create an independent unit within his agency to undertake all risk assessments. He did not want the scientific study of the dangers associated with certain substances and policies to be mixed with what he saw as political judgments about the acceptability of such risks or the best ways of managing them. He ultimately abandoned this view, publicly recanting the feasibility and the desirability of such a course.[6] Instead, Ruckelshaus now believes that science should be given its due, but not by isolating the scientists from the scrutiny of those who are politically accountable, and not by pretending that problem definition, fact-finding, bargaining, or treaty adjustment are "value-free" tasks that ought to be left solely to scientists.

What, then, does it mean to give science its due in a highly politicized context like international treaty negotiation? The experience of drafting the London Dumping Convention illustrates how sensitive this question can become, beginning with the problem of selecting scientific advisers. The convention regulates the release of low-level radioactive wastes into the ocean, but it calls for continual review of the original ban on the dumping of low-level radioactive wastes. The signatories to the basic 1972 treaty had a great deal of difficulty agreeing on the selection of experts to advise them. Some countries, led by the United Kingdom, proposed that the International Atomic Energy Association (IAEA) and the International Council of Scientific Unions (ICSU) select experts to review the evidence and make recommendations to the parties. Another group, led by Canada and Nauru, believed that the experts should instead be chosen directly by the parties, and that the panel should reflect the distribution of interests and regions among the signatories. As a compromise, the factions agreed to a two-stage review: first, a panel of twenty-two international experts nominated by ICSU and IAEA would prepare a report, then this document would be considered by an expanded panel, including representatives of governments and international organizations.[7]

The United States, Denmark, and Spain (along with nongovernmental organizations like Greenpeace International) submitted questions that they insisted be addressed by the panel, knowing full well that how the questions are framed would have a lot to do with the final content of the report. When an ad hoc working group was unable to consolidate the written questions, all submittals were passed along to the panel. At their meeting in June 1985, the experts were unable to reach any conclusions to submit to the signatories. So, the parties had to reconsider the moratorium on the disposal of low-level radioactive wastes without any clear recommendations from their scientific advisers.

The nations of the South Pacific wanted the ban to be permanent. They were concerned about Japan's plans to dump more than half a million barrels of radioactive wastes in the South Pacific. The United States was reluctant to accept the ban. In the end, Spain secured twenty-five votes (with six opposed and seven abstaining) for its motion to continue the ban pending (1) further consideration of the comparative risks of land-based disposal; and (2) proof that ocean dumping of radioactive wastes would not result in negative impacts on human health or cause significant damage to the marine environment. Such findings, of course, will be acceptable only if they are submitted by experts viewed as legitimate by all the parties. In short, giving science its due depends on the selection of experts credible to all the stakeholders.

It is rare when science drives politics, rather than the reverse. The Montreal Protocol negotiations suggest, though, that this is possible. From the point at which stratospheric ozone depletion was discovered, through the subsequent agreement by the signatories to ban CFCs and certain other ozone-depleting chemicals, science was a driving force behind the political actions that were taken. Four major scientific discoveries shaped the political debate: the initial CFC–ozone depletion hypothesis; the discovery of the ozone hole over Antarctica; the discovery of evidence linking the hole with CFCs; and the development of substitutes.[8]

The first discovery, the theory that CFCs might be linked to ozone depletion, led to the banning of aerosols in the United States and, ultimately, to the 1985 Vienna Convention on Substances That Deplete the Ozone Layer. Discovery of the ozone hole heightened political awareness and encouraged greater funding of research into its possible causes. When two rival theories emerged about the causes of the hole, a political rift developed. Countries that supported CFC limitations and those that opposed them used the theoretical disagreement to push their own political agenda. Eventually, science played a large role in bringing about political compromise; the development of substitutes for CFCs enabled politicians who opposed an outright ban to soften their stand. Throughout the CFC negotiations, scientists played a more important part than usual.

The Montreal Protocol contained a major political innovation that allowed for adjustments as new scientific data became available. Specifically, Article 6 requires that "beginning in 1990, and at least every four years thereafter, the parties shall assess the control measures on the basis of available scientific, environmental, technical and economic information. At least one year before each assessment, the parties shall convene appropriate panels of experts qualified in the fields mentioned and determine the composition and terms of reference of any such panels." The importance of this provision quickly became apparent. Two weeks after the Montreal Protocol negotiations were concluded, the results of a second National Ozone Expedition provided evidence that the situation was even worse than the negotiators had imagined.[9] The expedition documented the low-temperature chemical reaction that broke down CFCs into ozone-depleting chlorine. Things went quickly after that. A Helsinki conference of the parties to the protocol in May 1989 proposed amendments to be finalized at the first four-year review conference in 1990. The Helsinki conference also issued a declaration of intent to stop production and use of CFCs by the year 2000. The parties met in London, in 1990, as required by the protocol.

As British international relations expert Caroline Thomas (1992) describes it, the London conference had several aims: to amend the targets for CFC reductions and to look at the possibility of controls on other ozone-depleting substances; and to achieve wider adherence to the Montreal Protocol by persuading developing countries that had not yet joined to do so. The conference finally decided on a total phaseout by the year

2000, even though some countries wanted to move even more quickly. The conference called for a total phaseout of halons by 2000, and a phaseout of carbon tetrachloride by the same date. The target for the phaseout of methyl chloroform was set at the year 2005. As Thomas reports, no legal controls were set on the production or use of HCFCs, the most popular class of substitutes (with ozone-depleting and global-warming potentials of their own). The main political debate at the London conference was over the incentives to developing countries to join (that is, how much additional money, the mechanism through which the money would be allocated, and the ground rules regarding technology transfer).

In two decades of debate over ozone depletion, the focus was on scientific rather than political issues. Scientists consistently played a key role within national delegations, and international scientific organizations were prominent advisers. All of this was unusual. The discovery of the hole in the ozone layer (confirming the earlier scientific hypothesis) came as close to a "smoking gun" in scientific terms as is ever available. It established the environmental danger and its source. The provision of the protocol providing for scheduled joint fact-finding was clearly also an important factor in elevating the significance of scientific input. Finally, the availability of substitutes meant that politicians could give science its due without suffering major political losses. Even in the ozone depletion case, however, finding a balance between science and politics did not mean isolating one from the other.

## Adversary Science Undermines Trust

"Adversary science" poses the greatest danger to effective collaboration in response to global environment threats. If nations and the general public believe that scientists abuse the trust they place in them—when one so-called expert says yes and an equally distinguished expert says no—science will have no standing in environmental negotiations. That is, if anyone can instruct a scientist what to say on his or her behalf, and to bend the available scientific methods and evidence to suit his or her political objectives, then the scientific community will be nothing more than another political interest group casting its lot with one coalition or another. At that point, any argument that one definition of the problem or one approach to its resolution ought to be favored on technical grounds will rightly fall on deaf ears.

In a lawsuit (at least in the United States), everyone expects legal advocates to do everything they can to prove their client's case. The public is not surprised when competing experts are brought in to testify by the defense and the prosecution. These experts are obviously selected because of what they will say. Indeed, they are carefully coached before being brought to the witness stand so that embarrassing admissions can be avoided. No one expects such experts to be impartial. Using this approach as a model for involving experts in decision making, however, will undermine rather than strengthen global environmental negotiations.

Advocacy is not the same thing as bias. Scientists who work for nongovernmental organizations are often known, for example, to have a proenvironmental bias, but their work is still widely respected. The same is true of some scientists who work for industry. Their integrity is not necessarily suspect; that is, just because they work for industry does not mean they would knowingly disregard evidence just because it was contrary to the positions they or their employer had previously expressed. There is no reason to believe that these individuals would fabricate data or perjure themselves. Indeed, as scientists they would undermine their credibility and long-term career prospects if they engaged in such practices.

The CITES Convention (as it relates to African elephants) contains several institutional mechanisms designed to help the parties avoid conflicts between scientists. Most significant is the provision calling for the secretariat to serve as a screen or filter. The secretariat has responsibility for undertaking scientific and technical studies required for the convention's implementation. Much of this work is contracted out to NGOs. On the basis of this information, the secretariat makes recommendations to the parties to the convention (and disseminates reports received). Because the secretariat is viewed as a disinterested party looking for believable information, the fact that it screens the work coming from the NGOs is sufficient to establish the reliability of the data provided.

Several other practical approaches can be taken to counteract the potential impact of advocacy science on treaty negotiations. Such strategies for building or rebuilding trust emphasize counterweights to advocacy science, including the use of representative bodies of scientists (nominated by different coalitions); multitiered scientific advisory groups (with one layer made up of international scientific organizations and others comprising national scientific designees); mandatory meetings at which new scientific information is presented to the parties for their consideration; and, as is the case with the CITES Convention, reliance on a secretariat to screen and assemble credible scientific input. These strategies of course, are not mutually exclusive.

When scientists disagree, it does not mean they have nothing to contribute. There are many legitimate sources of scientific disagreement. Sometimes scientists working from different sets of data about the same phenomenon reach different conclusions. Often, experts from different disciplines are actually working on different aspects of the same problem but do not realize it. Although they may disagree in characterizing the problem, it may just be a matter of time before someone realizes how to put the pieces together to produce an even more powerful depiction or explanation. Depending on the standard of proof that individual experts require, one might say that the available evidence indicates one thing, while another says that it does not. They are, in fact, looking at the same findings but interpreting them differently. If the sources of scientific disagreement can be clarified, conflicting presentations can help enrich the public's understanding of the risks and the merits of alternative responses. This presumes, though, that scientists themselves will always be open to new evidence or interpretations that disconfirm their biases or strongly held beliefs.

## Are There Really "Epistemic Communities" of Scientists?

Another view about the interconnection between science and politics was presented by Peter Haas in his detailed study of efforts to control marine pollution in the Mediterranean Sea (1990). Haas attributes the success of that regional effort to "the involvement of ecologists and marine scientists who set the international agenda and directed their own states' support of international efforts and toward the introduction of strong pollution control measures at home." He calls this group of like-minded government officials, scientists, and secretariat members from specialized international agencies an "epistemic community" (that is, an informally coordinated lobbying group with a shared belief in ecological principles, similar views about the origins and severity of pollution, and the same ideas about the policies needed to control pollution). According to Haas, this scientific coalition coordinated a political effort to encourage governments to cooperate actively and intervene domestically to protect the Mediterranean environment.

Haas asserts that these midlevel government officials (from a variety of backgrounds), with only modest support from UNEP, had sufficient scientific prestige and motivation to separate themselves from their domestic political bases. That is, when consulted by their governments, these scientists provided policy advice about domestic pollution control measures and encouraged their countries to support the norms and principles contained in the Mediterranean Action Plan, whether or not their individual country's political interests were entirely met.

Haas talks about the role that epistemic communities can play in both the early problem-setting stages of multilateral policy-making and in encouraging their countries to comply with treaties (or regimes) once they are enacted. He equates compliance with the adoption of national policies consonant with the regime's norms. His explanation is that "if a group with a common perspective is able to acquire and sustain control over a substantive policy domain, the associated regime will become strong and countries will comply with it." Even though he does not have equally detailed case studies of the Montreal Protocol, the Long-Range Transboundary Air Pollution Convention, or the U.S.-Canadian acid rain negotiations to back him up, Haas conjectures that in these negotiations as well, ecological epistemic communities probably played important roles. Because his analysis has received a great deal of attention in the international relations field, it is important to consider it carefully.

Assume for a moment that Haas is right—that transnational epistemic communities can play an important part in shaping the way problems and policies are defined in global environmental treaty making. To my way of thinking, this is worrisome. First, it would mean that an ad hoc group of mostly appointed bureaucrats, no different from any other coalition of nonelected actors, had achieved disproportionate influence over crucial global decisions. And, although these happened to be trained scientists, assigned by their country to work on specific treaties, they did not feel bound to represent their national interests.

Those who favor the elimination of national sovereignty in favor of a broader commitment to the "heritage of mankind" might well be buoyed by Haas's findings. If he is right, there is a group with substantial influence that is not bound by traditional national loyalties. To the extent he is right, though, his story is likely to cause a boomerang effect. If, indeed, scientists assigned by governments to participate in environmental treaty making use their scientific prestige and transnational networks to usurp control over policymaking, they are bound to be reined in, if not banned, by their governments. Moreover, in the process of replacing them, elected leaders are more likely than ever to insist that the work of scientists be confined to less intrusive data-gathering activities, or, still worse, that only scientists who will advocate the national "party line" be appointed. That kind of "instructed science" would further undermine public support for scientific input in global environmental treaty making.

Let us hope that Haas has the story wrong. Indeed, as I. William Zartman suggests, "The much-vaunted epistemic community is a result rather than a motor of environmental negotiations."[9] To the extent that transnational coalitions or lobby groups emerge, whether of scientists, business interests, or nongovernmental groups, they tend to form in response to national coalitions that exist and not in advance of them. Moreover, I doubt very much whether the kind of epistemic community that Haas describes would have the clout to alter the balance of power between proponent coalitions and veto blocks. As Zartman says, "The transnational cooperation of scientists, technologies, and business illustrates one type of coalition that could be built as a basis for an environmental bargain, but it is generally not enough." Scientific coalitions can use their resources—knowledge, skill, and money—to raise consciousness, but they must enlist political leaders accountable to constituent groups to have a real impact on treaty negotiations. And such leaders are going to put domestic political considerations above the interests of scientific coalition.

In the climate change negotiations there is, at best, a fragmented epistemic community. While the International Panel on Climate Change (IPCC) was seeking to knit together a scientific consensus on the scope of the global warming problem and the appropriate response, scientists who disagreed with the majority of the technical fraternity were seeking to disrupt the consensus-building effort. Although many atmospheric-change scientists agreed to some version of the "greenhouse problem," the agreement fell apart when the scientists attempted to prescribe appropriate policy responses. And this is where I think Haas's model breaks down: it may be possible to win transnational approval for a general statement of a problem or a rough causal model of the sources of a global threat (especially when there is the equivalent of a smoking gun, like a hole in the ozone layer), but it is highly unlikely that a coalition of independent actors without national interests to defend will agree on a policy response, or that they will compete effectively for political support against national clusters that know their interests well. Haas may be right that cross-cutting scientific coalitions can help to encourage compliance with international treaties (in ways that supplement the work of other nongovernmental groups playing similar roles), but his claims for the formidable influence of epistemic communities in the formulation and enactment of global environmental treaties seem farfetched.

Moreover, it would be disastrous if scientists became nothing more than just another interest group pushing their own agenda. That would feed all the anxieties (especially in the South) regarding the use of technological sophistication as a means of exploitation. What we need, instead, are multilateral fact-finding efforts that seek to compile multiple perspectives on a problem or a threat and to clarify sources of disagreement among experts and disciplines. What we need is for domestic scientific advisers to adopt a Janus-like posture: helping to build understanding of the consequences of technical findings within their countries while maintaining their external ties to independent scientific organizations that can vouch for the adequacy of important scientific findings. Elected leaders and nongovernmental organizations should hold scientists accountable for maintaining this dual perspective: looking forward to building cooperation with their international peers but looking "backward" to take account of national priorities. Thus, scientists, too, must work to maintain a balance between technical and political considerations.

## Ongoing Roles for Scientific Advisers

Scientific advisers play at least five roles in the environmental treaty-making process. They are trend spotters, theory builders, theory testers, science communicators, and applied-policy analysts. The same scientists or scientific organizations can play several roles, and it does not matter whether their institutional home is a university or independent research center, international governmental organization, national government agency, nongovernmental organization, or corporation. Balance is best achieved by encouraging scientists working in each of these settings to confront one another in public forums as well as professional settings. Such interactions should be facilitated by umbrella organizations or skilled conveners used to managing such confrontations and making them understandable to the public. Interactions of this sort are needed at each phase of the negotiations on any global environmental treaty.

Trend spotters concern themselves primarily with documenting shifting ecological patterns in the biosphere. To do this, they must collect time-series data in a highly consistent fashion. Some groups specialize in reinterpreting data, such as the data collected for other purposes by the (LANDSAT) worldwide satellite flyovers. Other trend spotters collect their own primary data on a continuing basis. Unfortunately many time series do not go back far enough to highlight important changes taking place in geological time; other efforts to track important perturbations are hamstrung by missing data, inconsistent measurements, or data at too coarse a grain to allow microanalysis (that is, subnational analysis). The key problem for trend spotters is to be able to detect changes in ecological patterns and to understand when they are important.

Theory builders come from many disciplines. Their task is to explain the causes of the changes that the trend spotters identify. Using basic disciplinary knowledge and pushing it further to explain why patterns we have not seen before are occurring (and what their effects may be), theory builders try to fit explanations to past circumstances and to model likely futures.

Theory testers conduct experiments, that is, they organize expeditions or monitor natural or manmade inconsistencies that offer opportunities to test the hypotheses and propositions put forward by the theory builders. Sometimes they can mount pilot tests or experiments to see whether, under controlled circumstances, theoretical predictions actually occur. Some devote themselves to organizing experiments for the first time; others seek to replicate or validate prior results through repeated or related testing.

Communicators take responsibility for making the work of the first three types of scientists understandable to a larger audience. They may themselves engage in one of the first three types of work, but they specialize in writing or preparing material for the popular press or television. Their particular skill rests on an ability to translate scientific methods and findings into terms that the public at large can understand. Some journalists with technical backgrounds perform this role well, but the most effective scientific communicators tend to be highly trained individuals who have developed the knack of simplifying the complex mysteries of science, and who do not believe that their technical status is diminished by doing this kind of work. Activists and "monkey wrenchers" who engage in public confrontations aimed at focusing attention on scientific issues are playing important communicating roles. But, to the extent they are not willing to engage their nonactivist colleagues in a sustained technical dialogue, they fail to add much to improving the balance between science and politics in environmental treaty making.

Applied-policy analysts go beyond the interpretation of theoretical findings to the formulation of prescriptive advice, presumably as consultants to decision makers. Their prescriptions are not based on personal or ideological agendas but, rather, draw on the application of decision-analytic tools and techniques from the policy sciences (for example, applied economics, psychology, organizational behavior, and political science). Policy analysts must be able to formulate multiple courses of action and argue effectively for all of them.

All five types of scientists have roles to play in problem identification. Trend spotters and theory testers are usually more prominent during fact-finding. Science communicators and policy analysts have key roles to play during bargaining, especially as part of national delegations. And, all five types have a role to play in monitoring efforts aimed at treaty tightening. Ideally, teams of scientists (including all five types) will stay with a treaty-making effort as it evolves. This will better allow decision makers to hold them accountable for their analyses and predictions. It also means that the accumulation of evidence can be handled efficiently because at least part of each team will not need to start at ground zero every time new data or theories emerge. New scientific recruits are always needed, but familiarity with earlier documentation and debates is important.

Scientists need to be brought into the informal and formal networks surrounding each treaty-making effort with a clear sense of their obligations. The key is to bring together not only each of the five types of scientists at each step in the process, but to force them to confront the sources of their disagreements. Although this has traditionally been done behind the scenes, through the peer-review process associated with professional publications and conferences, it needs to be done publicly if the contributions of the scientific community are to have credibility. Such interactions need to be facilitated by skilled neutrals who can make the presentation of scientific controversies productive.[10]

The forums at which scientists are brought together must have ground rules. Procedures governing the gathering of scientific evidence and the conduct of scientific meetings have, from time to time, been built into certain treaties, but these have rarely been crafted with an eye toward ensuring a more effective ongoing relationship between technical and political actors. Instead, they have assumed that the scientists should meet first and reach agreement on the facts, and then let the politicians take over. What we need are guidelines that encourage continuing accountable relationships.

## No Regrets and the Precautionary Principle

Whatever the level of scientific uncertainty surrounding a treaty negotiation, there may be a simple way of proceeding that both politicians and scientists can support. That is, the parties should first try to find a "no-regrets" approach to the problem. The trick is to identify a course of action that generates benefits for all stakeholders, regardless of whether or not they agree with the theory of the problem or believe that the proposed solution will be effective. For instance, in the debate over global warming, encouraging all nations to adopt low-cost energy conservation measures would constitute a no-regrets approach. If the United States burned less fossil fuel to produce electricity, the emission of greenhouse gases would be cut. Even if a country does not agree that atmospheric warming is occurring at a problematic rate, there are sufficient cost savings associated with greater energy efficiency to make it a policy worth pursuing. If further study shows that global warming is, indeed, occurring as a result of $CO_2$ emissions, then the adoption of low-cost, energy-saving strategies will have helped combat the problem. If, instead, it turns out that the ocean's absorptive capacities or misunderstood atmospheric dynamics give us a much greater margin for $CO_2$ increases than we thought, the nation will still have saved a substantial amount of money by conserving fuel.

There are other no-regrets approaches to handling global environmental threats that even scientists who disagree strongly with one another's theories or forecasts could agree upon. The pollution prevention idea currently being pursued by many large corporations is a good example. The concept is simple: While attempting to comply with tougher pollution emission regulations, some industries have found new materials or production processes that reduce pollution levels and increase productivity (and sometimes save money) as well. They not only have found cost-effective substitutes (and profitable new uses for recycled byproducts) that reduce the volume of pollutants requiring disposal but also have discovered new production methods that help to increase their market share by establishing an improved (that is, "greener") public image. Corporate managers continue to search for more cost-effective ways of avoiding pollution by making still other changes in production. This no longer involves a grudging response to tougher environmental regulation; rather, industries are exploring, without any regrets, ways of meeting regulatory responsibilities that increase savings.

One step beyond the no-regrets approach is the precautionary principle. As presented in the Rio Declaration (Principle 15) it reads: "In order to protect the environment, the precautionary approach shall be widely applied by States according to their capabilities. Where there are threats of serious or irreversible damage, lack of full scientific certainty shall not be used as a reason for postponing cost-effective measures to prevent environmental degradation." This is something that most scientists can endorse.

Although referenced in numerous international legal documents, the precautionary principle is not yet part of (customary) international law. As Porter and Brown describe it, the principle "would shift the burden of proof from opponents of a given activity that could degrade the environment to those engaged in the activity in question. Thus, the principle would require potential polluters to establish that substances to be released into the environment would not damage it, with procedures for systematic assessment and documentation as well as public access to information and to the decisionmaking process."

Michael Jacobs, in *The Green Economy* (1992), suggests that the world is faced with two possible courses of action: controlling environmental effects and not controlling them. Shall we act as if the climatologists are correct in predicting that current trends will cause catastrophic changes in living patterns? Our decision ought to depend on the probability we attach to their being right and their being wrong. One reasonable response, consistent with the precautionary principle, is to act in ways aimed at minimizing our maximum cost. As Jacobs points out, most people are not tempted by gambles in which their losses could be very large, however great the possible gains. A policy of minimizing the maximum cost (on the assumption that the predicted costs of global warming are considerably greater than the costs of controlling emissions) would lead us to opt for $CO_2$ emission controls.

Some analysts, particularly economists, argue that all we need to do (in order to make smart decisions) is to calculate the expected value of each of the two courses of action that Jacobs describes. This involves calibrating the monetary value of a great many factors that are all but impossible to quantify. Indeed, given the hopelessness of such a approach, it may make more sense to turn to the emerging discipline of ecological economics. This new approach to economic analysis offers innovative methods for managing uncertainty and measuring environmental quality. It also offers insights into the intelligent application of the precautionary principle, which in its naive interpretation seems to entail a halt to all innovation, but which, as this new discipline shows, calls for "the management of the burden of proof in a disciplined and standardized way."[11]

Ecological economics puts a premium on the kind of pluralistic dialogue among political actors and scientific experts that I have described. It is organized around the precautionary principle, although it also owes its existence to another principle, that of sustainable development. Ecological economics presumes that it is possible to compare the "relative sustainability" of alternative development strategies without monetizing everything or discounting to zero the interests of future generations, the way that neoclassical economics requires. Although the methods of sustainability analysis (described in Chapter 3) still need to be developed further, they hold much greater promise than cost-benefit analysis.[12] The precautionary principle and the principle of sustainable development, plus the pragmatic search for no-regrets alternatives whenever possible, offer an intellectual framework for balancing science and politics in global environmental treaty making.

## Contingent Agreements Are the Answer

Even if the precautionary principle were mandated by international law and the participants in global environmental treaty negotiations adopted a no-regrets strategy whenever possible, political disagreements would still emerge. They would often be sustained by self-serving claims about the dangers of acting in the face of scientific uncertainty. One response to these claims emphasizes a stepwise push toward greater certainty through the adoption of weak framework conventions coupled with a substantial investment in joint research, careful monitoring, and progressive treaty tightening.

Relying on contingent agreements, however, may make it possible to move further and faster. Contingent agreements sidestep the need for consensus on what the future holds or which policy responses are likely to be most effective. Instead of settling for a broad framework convention without targets or deadlines, the parties to a treaty negotiation could spell out—at the time a framework is debated—contingent actions that would come into force if certain events occurred or thresholds were passed. In other words, the parties would negotiate multiple protocols that could contain mutually contradictory requirements. Not all of these would take effect. As measurements came in, it would be clear which protocols would apply. This would not eliminate the need for continued treaty monitoring and tightening (in fact, it would make monitoring even more important), but it would produce more effective agreement even when there was substantial scientific uncertainty. If nothing else, the lowest-common-denominator approach to treaty making could be avoided.

Developing contingent agreements is not the same thing as negotiating a framework convention and then waiting to see if there is support for subsequent protocols. Rather, it is an alternative to the two-step process on which the United Nations has relied for the past two decades. The alternative "if-then" format I am describing need not be overly complicated, and the number of contingent options or protocols need not be large. For example, in future negotiations over the protection of forests, multiple protocols could be negotiated and signed at the same time as a framework convention. The first protocol, calling for substantial restrictions on the cutting of virgin or old-growth forests would come into effect only if a certain threshold of worldwide forest losses was passed. The second protocol with far fewer restrictions, would remain in effect unless or until the first protocol was triggered.

Multiple protocols would allow the parties to sidestep differences in their forecasts and causal explanations of the risks. They would still be able to pursue no-regret options, and respect the precautionary principle. They would not do this by taking the least risky course of action; instead, they would spell out exactly what their commitments would be under varying sets of circumstances.

The argument against the use of contingent agreements is basically that they would, at least in the early stages, require more extensive (and perhaps more complicated) negotiations. This time would be made up, though, by eliminating the need to negotiate subsequent protocols (although, again, treaty tightening based on monitoring and follow-up research would still be necessary). The use of contingent agreements would guarantee subsequent action beyond a general framework convention—something we cannot count on now. It would also reduce the debilitating effect of advocacy science in the early stages of problem definition because complete scientific consensus would not be necessary. Finally, a contingent approach would force scientists to be much more precise about the goals of joint monitoring and collaborative research. The gains would be substantial, and a much better balance between science and politics would be achieved.

# CHAPTER 5

# The Advantages and Disadvantages of Issue Linkage

Most global environmental treaty making involves hundreds of negotiators in a dialogue sustained over many years that covers literally thousands of complex issues. Unfortunately, most of the published theoretical work about negotiation presumes just two parties negotiating a single issue, or two adversaries negotiating on a continuing basis. In addition, most negotiation theorists focus on monolithic parties: individuals who can speak for themselves and make binding commitments. The parties in global environmental treaty making, however, are anything but monolithic. Indeed, even when the parties are heads of state, they must seek the advice and/or consent of others (typically their parliament or congress) to ratify a treaty that legally commits their country. An expanded theory of negotiation, one that takes into account the fact that nonmonolithic parties negotiate a series of linked issues, is sorely needed to deal with global environmental treaty making.

The few scholars who have written about multiparty, multi-issue negotiation point out that (1) it is much more difficult to initiate complex negotiations of this sort than traditional two-party negotiations because of the sheer number of people whose concerns and schedules must be coordinated; (2) it is much more difficult to fix an agenda or know when acceptable agreements have been reached because of internal conflict within stakeholding groups; and (3) it typically requires elaborate management on the part of a strong, but neutral, facilitator or chair to hammer out an efficient agreement. In all three instances, linkage—trading across what appear to be completely different realms—can be crucial to the success of the negotiation.

One way of bringing a reluctant party to the bargaining table is to guarantee that an issue about which it is greatly concerned will be on the agenda; indeed, it may have to be accorded a privileged place, high on the roster of issues, to provide a sufficient incentive to join. For example, China and India, before they would join in the Montreal Protocol negotiations, insisted that a major focus of the talks had to be the issue of additional financial aid from the North to the South (as well as Southern access to Northern technology).

Although linkage can help bring reluctant parties to the table, it can also make it more difficult to reach agreement. As the agenda is enlarged, an increasing array of domestic interests will want or need to be consulted, making each stakeholding party's job more complicated. Particularly when issues are added to the agenda at the last minute, in an effort to close a remaining gap, the seeds of opposition can be planted. Opposition tends to emerge during formal ratification, when groups that believe they were left out demand a chance to be heard. Such groups may even have chosen not to participate in the negotiation because the agenda did not interest them, but when it changed at the last minute, their interests may well have been adversely affected. These parties have a legitimate argument when they say that they were left out, even if it seemed utterly impractical to bring them in so late in the game.

When impasse looms because no party is willing to back down from its initial demands, one of the ways in which skilled mediators forge agreement is by privately assuring one side (based on confidential communications with the others) that a trade is possible. If Party A believes it will get what it wants on issue 1 (its highest priority), then it may well grant Party B what it requires on issue 2 (B's highest priority). By exploiting the fact that the parties value the two issues differently, the mediator often finds it possible to construct agreements that are better for all sides than no agreement.

The mechanics of this kind of issue linkage can be daunting. Imagine hundreds of parties trying to influence the construction of an agenda or the packaging of issues during a negotiation. No party wants to advocate an issue too eagerly for fear that its support for that issue will be used against it by others. If I want something very much and you know it, you may be able to use that information to demand more from me than you would otherwise be able to get—at least that is the way that most people think about negotiation. To overcome this problem and avoid a stalemate (in which no party wants to reveal which issues are of greatest importance to it or what it is really willing to accept on each issue), a neutral party needs to meet privately with each stakeholding group. By playing the game of "what if . . ." on a confidential basis with each party, a neutral can construct an agenda or propose "packages" that all parties can accept with none having to announce its true priorities. Absent such intervention, it is unlikely that the parties in a multilateral negotiation will reach an efficient agreement, one that maximizes joint gains.

The research on multiparty negotiation suggests that it is important to know the answers to the following questions: When does it help to add an issue or a party, and when does expanding the agenda or the assembly make it even more difficult to reach agreement? Which kinds of linkages are legitimate, and which are counterproductive? How can treaty negotiators avoid inviting blackmail while still exploiting the advantages of issue linkage? Won't issue linkage add to the (already considerable) institutional complexity of treaty negotiations, and bog down the process?

Before looking again at the accords discussed in Chapter 1 for more specific answers to these questions, it may be instructive to review the ongoing progress of one of the most remarkable instances of international issue linkage: "debt-for-nature swaps." These do not take the precise form of multilateral treaties, but they have many of the same characteristics (that is, many parties must negotiate many issues requiring national governments to make environment-development trade-offs).

Early debt-for-nature swaps typically involved two types of transactions. The first was a negotiation among an international environmental organization, a debtor government, and its central bank about the desirability of linking debt reduction to resource conservation or environmental protection. The second involved local conservation groups and focused on the details of environmental protection agreements. Most early swaps began when an international environmental organization bought a country's foreign debt from a creditor institution, usually at a greatly discounted price. The debt note was retraded with the national government, often at full face value. Then, the government issued local currency bonds to finance long-term conservation efforts. Once this was completed, a local conservation group worked with representatives of the national forestry or park ministries and the international environmental group to devise detailed conservation plans. In most cases, the local conservation organization subcontracted with numerous local nongovernmental organizations to implement the details of the agreement.

The first debt-for-nature swap was concluded in 1987, when Bolivia established three "buffer zones" totaling 3.7 million acres adjacent to the existing 135,000-acre Beni Biosphere Reserve in the Andes foothills (Dawkins, 1990). A $250,000 local currency fund was set aside to cover long-term conservation management in the area. In exchange, Conservation International purchased $650,000 worth of Bolivian debt at a price of $100,000, (an 85 percent discount on the face value of the debt). In 1987 swaps were also negotiated with Ecuador and Costa Rica. Debt was purchased in these instances at discount rates of 65 percent and 85 percent. In 1989 swaps were completed with the Philippines, Zambia, and Madagascar, the last of which included the participation of the U.S. Agency for International Development.

A new generation of swaps has since developed. Bilateral and multilateral institutions have begun to express interest in acting as intermediaries, or offering credit enhancements in the form of "conservation exit bonds" for existing debt or "green bonds" for new loans. Conservation exit bonds are used by multilateral development banks to help restructure debt. If a bank agrees to a debt swap, it can get credit in the form of a guarantee that improves the value of the banks' other debt (in proportion to the amount donated). Green bonds offer something similar: credit enhancements to banks agreeing to incur new debt in the form of bonds designated for financing conservation.

In addition, the most recent swaps have emphasized government-to-government transactions of a much larger scale. The Paris Club (seventeen countries including the United States) has agreed to a debt-for-nature swap that, if fully implemented, would provide more than $3.3 billion to help clean up Poland's environment. The Polish plan provides for 100 percent of this forgiveness to be paid in local currency to finance environmental programs. This was on top of $35 billion of external debt that was also forgiven by the same countries to reward Poland for its economic reform programs and to help support the democratically elected Solidarity government.[1]

In debt-for-nature swaps, two distinct issues—the environment and debt—are linked. As with the linkage of any issues, combining them increases the scope of the negotiations but also increases the complexity and the risk of failure. Moreover, the political sensitivity of the dependency implied by foreign debt makes debt-for-nature swaps particularly controversial. Nevertheless, it is clear that linking the two issues has helped to promote environmental protection in countries that would otherwise have refused to take the issue seriously. In sum, debt-for-nature swaps have succeeded because environmental concerns have supplied the necessary momentum while debt relief has provided the means for resolving a conflict of international interests.

Debt-for-nature swaps have not been without their detractors. From the standpoint of some political observers, these swaps are nothing less than a new form of "ecocolonialism."[2] "Foreigners" from the North, whose industrial economies grew by damaging the planet's delicate ecosystems, now seek to solve "their" environmental problems by limiting development in the South. They are doing this, the critics assert, by exploiting economic dependency that the North itself created by offering loans on terms that developing countries could not possibly meet. Furthermore, the critics contend, by manipulating interest rates and capital flows, the North has caused rapid inflation, making it impossible for the South to pay back what it owes. Meanwhile, the North continues to lend money to the developing world (at high interest rates), preventing poor debtor nations from using their trade revenues to develop economically, while demanding more of the South's natural resources at lower prices.

Some debtor nations assert that their accumulated debts are illegitimate because they were negotiated by despotic military regimes or forced on them by the International Monetary Fund as a precondition for other kinds of assistance. In short, the critics question the fundamental legitimacy of these international debts, arguing, for the most part, that all old debt ought to be forgiven.

Whether the long-term debts of the South are legitimate or not, and whether international nongovernmental organizations ought to be meddling in the national budget priorities of the developing world are, by definition, matters for each country to decide. Bolivia's president, José Sarney, was initially skeptical about the 1988 proposed debt-for-nature swap. He argued that it was unfair to put pressure on Bolivia to take land out of development just to meet the environmental interests of the North. After hearing, though, that the swap would relieve his country of $650,000 of foreign debt, give it—not an international environmental group—the lead in making conservation decisions, and secure permanent funding for one of the largest conservation areas in the world, he signed the agreement.

In other debt-for-nature arrangements, the array of linked issues has been even broader. The Dutch government, for example, stipulated in its agreement with Costa Rica that debt originating in loans linked in any way to the purchase of arms would be excluded. Indigenous groups in some Latin American countries have proposed that debt-for-nature swaps should be contingent on the recognition of their territorial claims. There are even some groups that have suggested that debt-for-nature swaps should be used to combat the international drug trade by providing incentives to coca farmers to induce them to put their land into conservation. Although there is no intrinsic limit on the array or type of issues that can be linked in a multilateral negotiation, there are logistical problems and strategic considerations that can create barriers. In the final analysis, however, debt-for-nature swaps illustrate quite clearly that surprising interconnections can be made between issues that, under normal circumstances, would not be related. Parallel gains could be achieved by applying the linkage concept to the broader field of environmental diplomacy.

## A Lesson in Negotiation Arithmetic

Issue linkage can facilitate an international environmental negotiation in three ways. First, by adding an issue, one party can offer others additional advantages, and thus a reason to agree. Second, by adding an issue, and thereby bringing other parties to the bargaining table, it is also possible to counteract the power of a blocking coalition (by increasing the size of the coalition that favors agreement). Finally, adding an issue makes it possible to shift the institutional locus of a negotiation to a new venue in which implementation may be easier. Each of these uses of linkage involves building or modifying coalitions.

Howard Raiffa in *The Art and Science of Negotiation* (1982) and James Sebenius in *Negotiating the Law of the Sea* (1984) emphasize the importance of properly sequencing issue addition and subtraction.[3] As issues are added or taken away, not only does the number of parties change but strategic alliances are altered. If this is done purposefully, with the support of all the parties, it can make the difference between success and failure in global environmental treaty negotiations. If it happens in an unplanned way, or without the support of the key stakeholders, it can undermine the prospects of reaching agreement.

In general, the purpose of adding or subtracting issues (and parties) is to create "additional value." This is accomplished by exploiting the differing degrees of importance that each party attaches to the issues on a negotiation agenda. According to Raiffa and Sebenius, parties can "widen their zone of possible agreement" by adding new issues. They can strengthen a coalition or defeat a blocking coalition by adding or subtracting an issue. And, finally, they can strengthen the bargaining commitments of the parties by adding or subtracting issues. The next two sections will describe how each maneuver has affected past global environmental negotiations.

## Adding Issues

The Law of the Sea negotiations from 1975 to 1984 are the classic example of how to widen the zone of agreement through issue linkage. By adding deep seabed mining to the agenda of more traditional maritime issues, the Law of the Sea negotiators were able to create additional benefits to be shared, although the difficulty of their task increased as they added issues. The industrialized countries favored a system that would have allowed them to mine the seabed on a commercial basis. The developing countries wanted an "international body to be the sole exploiter of seabed resources." In either case, the mining of common seabed resources was, for many countries, tightly linked to other concerns regarding the use and control of the oceans. On the deep seabed mining issue, the parties were able to overcome an impasse by linking two issues on which they had deadlocked.

As Sebenius describes it, about 90 percent of the issues at the Law of the Sea conference had been settled, but several pivotal questions remained. One involved financial arrangements regarding the allocation of money collected by countries and corporations that would pay for the right to mine the ocean floor. On the question of fees, royalties, and profit sharing, the prospective mining countries, aware of the uncertainties surrounding deep seabed mining, wanted to pay low levels of profit based on flexible charges. Representatives of developing countries wanted payments to be high, fixed, and rigid. The same two groups also disagreed on how responsibility for the funding of a new international seabed authority should be assigned. The developing countries wanted a high proportion of long-term, interest-free loans. The developed countries wanted a system of loans that would supplement whatever the new entity could collect from commercial sources. This would reduce the amount that developed countries would be expected to contribute to start-up operations. By linking the two issues, that is, opting for a flexible system emphasizing long-term and interest-free loans, the impasse was overcome. Thus, the parties were able to conclude a bargain on two questions that, when treated one at a time, would have been irreconcilable.

The involvement of nonwhaling nations in the administration of the Whaling Treaty illustrates how adding parties can reduce the strength of a blocking coalition. The power of nonwhaling nations grew steadily during the 1970s, peaking in 1982 with the passage of the zero-quota for harvesting of all whale stocks (Stedman, 1990). Prior to that year, there were often times when this coalition gathered enough votes to block anticonservation efforts, but they had not been able to overcome the opposition of the whaling nations to a full moratorium on whaling.

Throughout the 1970s and early 1980s nonwhaling nations and conservation organizations attempted to persuade additional nonwhaling nations to join the International Whaling Commission so that they could obtain the three-quarters majority required to impose a moratorium. First there was an increase in the number of nations with observer (nonvoting) status at the IWC, from 5 in the mid-1970s to 11 by 1981. Slowly, the number of delegates (from both voting and observing nations) increased. Finally, by the time the zero-quota was passed, there were 190 delegates at the IWC meeting. During the 1970–1976 period, there had been an average of only seventy-seven delegates at each meeting. The number of delegates from nonwhaling nations increased more than eight and half times from 1970 to 1982, while those from whaling nations only doubled. Adding parties diluted the power of a blocking coalition.

The Montreal Protocol sought to strengthen the commitment of developing nations to eliminating CFC emissions by offering them compensation. The compensation consisted of funds administered through the World Bank (and later the Global Environmental Facility). Caroline Thomas (1992:234) points out that the Group of Seventy-seven nations might have done better had they based their request for compensation on the "polluter-pays" principle (that is, making a property rights claim on Northern funds equal to the damage caused by CFC emissions) rather than, as they did, demanding the "free" transfer of CFC alternatives. Thus, the Group of Seventy-seven demanded $350 million as the price for not producing CFCs, while full compensation for past damages might have "exceeded many times over the cost of new technology." Choosing the right issues to link is crucial.

## Subtracting Issues

A key reason to subtract issues is to make negotiations more manageable. There has been talk for years of a comprehensive "Law of the Atmosphere" approach to climate-change negotiations, paralleling the earlier Law of the Sea negotiations. The difficulties involved in that decade-long treaty-making effort, however, were enough to suggest that the costs of covering all aspects of climate change in one convention far outweighed the benefits of comprehensiveness.

Issue linkage helped to overcome some obstacles to agreement in the Law of the Sea negotiations, but the comprehensiveness of the treaty was one reason it was not formally ratified by the United States, Britain, and others. Although these countries liked much of what the treaty offered, they were unwilling to accept the proposed agreement on subseabed mining. The subtraction of issues is a means whereby winning coalitions can be held together.

The subtraction of an issue that in and of itself has no obvious zone of agreement from a larger array of questions allows support for a treaty to grow. The Climate Change Convention of 1992 did not produce an agreement on timetables and targets for the stabilization of $CO_2$ emissions, yet 152 countries did sign it. Many of the same parties were able to reach an agreement on phasing out CFCs that did include timetables and targets. The prospect of a carbon tax on energy production, however, was never seriously discussed in the context of the Montreal Protocol negotiations.

Had it been on the agenda as a means of financing CFC phaseouts (and had there not been readily available substitutes), I doubt that the Montreal Protocol would have been so widely supported.

It is possible for an elaborate agreement to fail because one too many issues was added to the negotiation. Expanding the array of issues can help open up the possibility of mutually beneficial trades, but negotiators quickly become aware of the dangers of taking on too much. In the final analysis, manageability is more important than the theoretical prospect of squeezing out additional joint gains.

It is important to note that adding and subtracting issues may not be effective on a treaty-by-treaty basis. In the future, it may be necessary to consider sets of treaties simultaneously, or even to look at individual treaties in the context of a larger North-South global bargain. Porter and Brown (1991:148) suggest that such a strategy might be part of a holistic approach, as opposed to the current incremental approach, to crafting environmental regimes. Even though it is doubtful that such a bargain could be worked out in a single conference or contained in a single agreement, it may well be that the North and the South need to encourage a new overarching partnership that links a variety of issues and principles in a metanegotiation.

A new North-South partnership might, for example, balance a commitment from the developing countries—especially Brazil, Mexico, China, and Indonesia—to make their economic development plans more responsive to the environmental concerns of the North, if the North, in turn, agrees to certain economic assistance, trade, and development objectives of importance to the South. The South, for instance, might promise to manage its resources more sustainably, work to curb population growth, share substantial responsibility for reducing the emission of greenhouse gases, and allow greater grass-roots participation in national environmental decision making. For its part, the North could pledge to end the drain of capital from developing countries (by increasing official development aid and forgiving debt), open its markets still further to manufactured goods from developing countries; provide access to advanced technologies on a concessionary basis; and curb wasteful high per capita consumption, especially of energy.

Some of these promises could be embodied in future agreements on sustainable development in which the North and the South make reciprocal commitments. Others might involve conditioning the completion of one agreement on the completion of others. For example, Porter and Brown suggest that the South might demand that the North reduce its per capita consumption of energy in exchange for limits on population growth in the South. This would mean that implementation of a future global

energy treaty might depend on successful completion of programs to reduce population growth levels in certain developing countries.

A new North-South bargain will have a chance of succeeding where
earlier efforts failed only if much more complicated policy linkages can be
achieved. Future environmental agreements will probably have to be
linked to explicit promises about financial flows, trade, and debt in ways
that have not occurred before. Negotiations over the General Agreement
on Tariffs and Trade, for example—as difficult as they already are—may
need to be linked to implementation of sustainable development and global resource management treaties.

## The Theory of Linkage

In 1979 former U.S. Secretary of State Henry Kissinger wrote:

> We insisted that progress in superpower relations, to be real, had to
> be made on a broad front. Events in different parts of the world, in our
> view, were related to each other; even more so, Soviet conduct in differ-
> ent parts of the world. We proceeded from the premise that to separate
> issues into distinct compartments would encourage the Soviet leaders to
> believe that they could use cooperation in one area as a safety value while
> striving for unilateral advantage elsewhere. This was unacceptable.[4]

Kissinger's advocacy of issue relationships "on a broad front" is another way of describing his support for the concept of linkage. The Soviets
denounced the policy. Every issue, Moscow argued, "ought to be settled
on its own merits," although when they wanted something badly enough
the Soviets, too, used linkage. Linkage is, in fact, a variation of the classic
political strategy of logrolling: "You give me something that I want very
much, and I will give you something important in exchange." Legislators
have always operated on this "you-scratch-my-back, I'll-scratch-your-
back" basis, but note, in most such situations they are exchanging things
that each one wants.

Linkage, as Kissinger practiced it, involved trading things that one
side wanted for concessions from the other side (for example, "no credits
and trade unless you let Soviet Jews emigrate"). One-sided trades do not
create value, although they may provide leverage for one side. The notion
of issue linkage, in negotiation theory, is more usefully thought of in terms
of trades that benefit both sides.

Nor is the idea of conditionality quite what negotiation theorists have
in mind when they speak about linkage. If-then statements that do not
increase the "size of the pie" may help one side, but are they do not "create
value." When participants in a negotiation link issues and make a package

that gives all participants more of what they want, they are adding to the total value of benefits to be allocated. The question, then, is what kinds of issue linkage are most helpful and which can get in the way of producing multilateral agreement. In his classic work on this subject, Ernst Haas (1985:374), talks about "linking issues into packages in deference to some intellectual strategy." He suggests that some functional connection is required to create a legitimate package, implying that utterly unrelated issues should not be linked because there is no causal nexus. He goes on to say that "knowledge (of a causal connection) can legitimate collaborative behavior *only* when the possibility of joint gains from the collaboration exists and is recognized." Thus, all negotiators must perceive an advantage (or at least no loss) for a proposed issue linkage to work. And the connection between otherwise unrelated issues must be acceptable to all the parties involved. In my view, identifying such causal connections and helping the parties accept them are key among the most important tasks of a mediator.

In all the best-known studies of continuing, as opposed to one-shot, negotiating relationships, cooperation evolves when the parties work to satisfy the interests of those with whom they are negotiating. Satisfaction, though, is a function of perceptions: "I will try to convince you that a particular package is good for you, but in the final analysis it only matters what you think, not what I think." So, some linkages or packages will be unacceptable to you because they do not have the same meaning for you that they do for me. Thus, linkage can help to close a gap between the parties in a treaty negotiation by creating additional benefits that one party can offer another. This will work, though, only if all parties perceive the trade as adding value for them. Moreover, there usually needs to be some sort of functional or causal connection between the issues to establish the legitimacy, which in such circumstances is entirely in the eyes of the beholder.

## Dealing with the Threat of Blackmail

There is always a risk that a package proposed by one side will be viewed as blackmail by another. The message conveyed by statements like "Unless you give me what I want on issue 1, I will not give you what you want on issue 2" is not a useful approach to linkage. Such a tactic—in effect, negative bargaining or threats—certainly does not create value in the eyes of both parties. Although it is possible, on occasion, for one side in a negotiation to gain certain advantages by making (believable) threats of this sort, there is a terrible price to pay in damaged relationships. In the case of environmental treaty making, winning support for a convention by extorting or blackmailing the other parties probably means that implementation will be doubly difficult as the reluctant parties then seek revenge. Extortion is a form of linkage with no justification other than force. From the standpoint of a party being blackmailed, the issue is not so much what is being offered but the fact that it has no attractive alternative and its rights are being abridged. Linkage that is not mutually agreeable always borders on blackmail.

There is a risk that constantly pushing to find additional value through linkages can create a climate that Roger Fisher describes as a "stingy bargaining environment"—in which each side always holds out for more, even after satisfying their fundamental interests. This stance can become self-defeating if the parties turn down "good" agreements that they actually have in hand in favor of theoretically superior outcomes. Some sort of ground rules that encourage the search for joint gains, while ruling out blackmail, and avoid an overly stingy bargaining environment are needed to guide global environmental treaty making. Mediators often spend considerable time helping the parties develop such ground rules. And, they play an important part in persuading the parties that the search for a still "better" agreement ought to come to an end.

Ground rules of this sort are what Roger Fisher and Scott Brown propose in *Getting Together* (1988); they are concerned about building good negotiating relationships. They focus on the key factors in establishing mutually satisfactory relationships. These include: *acceptance* ("deal with them seriously despite all differences"); *persuasion* ("rely on persuasion not coercion," "balance emotion with reason"); *reliability* ("be wholly trustworthy, not wholly trusting"); *communication* ("always consult before deciding"); *understanding* ("learn how they see things"); and *congruence* ("use the above elements so they are in harmony with each other.") I cannot think of any better advice to parties involved in global environmental treaty negotiations. Parties that will be dealing with each other on a continuing basis ought to interact in ways that make it easier rather than harder to deal with each other in the future. Indeed, they ought to put much more emphasis on strengthening their relationship than on short-term victories at the expense of others. Since global environmental treaty making brings the same countries together again and again, short-term victories at the expense of others are sure to make future negotiations much more difficult.

Issue linkage is consistent with Fisher and Brown's advice, if and only if packaging is done by mutual agreement. In addition, the parties in treaty negotiation have a right to expect benefits that would otherwise be rightfully theirs. Thus, it is not appropriate to remove (sovereign) rights, and then offer to restore them to countries that accept environmental treaties. Linkage should be used primarily to create additional joint gains that can be created in no other way and not as a means of threatening or depriving countries of benefits to which they are already entitled.

## Managing the Complexity

In the 1970s, the Group of Seventy-seven nations, with the approval of the United Nations General Assembly, began advocating its proposal for a "New International Economic Order" (NIEO). This proposed economic revolution followed a decade of debate on the future of North-South relations and still other UN efforts to formulate a worldwide economic development strategy. Although the North wanted no part of NIEO, the South has still not relinquished the objectives of the proposal: increased capital flows from North to South, greater technology sharing by the North with the South, lower Northern trade restrictions on industrialized products from the South, and guaranteed higher prices for raw materials exported from South to North. The General Assembly did approve a resolution calling on the industrialized nations to commit 0.7 percent of their gross national products to official development aid (ODA) each year, but the United States and several other major developed countries never accepted that target. Now, however, the debate about North-South relations and worldwide economic development strategy are intertwined with global efforts to achieve sustainable development. If the South makes meeting its earlier economic goals a quid pro quo for its willingness to participate in collective efforts to respond to environmental threats, all progress on the environmental front will come to a halt. If, however, the South's objectives can be linked strategically (perhaps *opportunistically* is a better word) with Northern efforts to achieve environmental protection and sustainable development, then the impetus for sustained global cooperation may finally be provided.

The creation of the Global Environmental Facility (GEF) and the willingness of the North to commit substantial amounts of additional development assistance to implement global environmental treaties represents a move in a new direction. Probably the greatest accomplishment of the 1992 Earth Summit was the expansion of the scope of the GEF's mandate and the little-noticed promise to modify its governing structure.[5] The money provided through the GEF must still be project-specific, but it is being offered as compensation; that is, it is supposed to cover the costs that developing countries will face in their efforts to meet the obligations outlined in the Montreal Protocol, Climate Change Convention, and other treaties. Money will be allocated for specific projects approved by the GEF's scientific advisory committee. With regard to the Climate Change

Convention, for example, developing countries might propose afforestation projects, energy conservation programs, or the building of new power-production facilities using environmentally friendly technologies. The GEF will work to ensure that all funded projects are consistent with the goal of reducing the emission of greenhouse gases. Of course, in deciding how to allocate $1 billion or more per year, the GEF will have to choose among a great many projects, all of which meet the minimal goals specified in the relevant treaties.

Critics of linkage arrangements like those exemplified by GEF assert there is little difference between compensation and bribery. As long as the North is convinced that the money flowing through the GEF is conditioned on the meeting of treaty requirements by countries and projects that pass technical muster, it will continue to pump in money. If the South, however, pushes too hard to remove all conditionality (for example, arguing that independent scientific review of proposed projects is inappropriate, or each developing country should be allocated GEF aid on the basis of need rather than on the basis of project proposals), the constructive linkage achieved thus far will be lost. The North will simply say no to continuing its contributions. The way to ensure the distinction between compensation and bribery is to ensure that both sides accept the legitimacy of the linkage. Furthermore, the GEF should only fund projects that have a chance of becoming institutionally and financially self-sustaining in the long term. The South will have to accept a certain level of conditionality and the North will have both to increase the amount of money the GEF has to allocate and to set minimum targets and standards for overall allocations to each developing nation or region.

In addition to the possibility that compensation will be confused with bribery, another risk posed by linkage is the creation of too much complexity. Whenever environmentalists suggest that global environmental treaty making ought to be linked to other negotiations, such as the General Agreement on Tariffs and Trade (GATT), the first response is that the complexity would be overwhelming. A closer look at the assertion, however, finds it is not convincing. GATT, drafted in 1947, regulates most world trade and is updated periodically. The current round of update negotiations, known as the Uruguay Round, was supposed to have been completed by December 1990 but continues on—plagued not by complexities caused by linking environmental concerns to world trade talks but by several conflicts including one between the United States and Europe over the appropriateness of agricultural production subsidies.

For much of the world, trade practices determine the way natural resources are used. Yet, GATT has been negotiated again and again with virtually no consideration of its environmental impacts or the oppor-

tunities it presents for reinforcing the important objectives of global environmental treaties. Part of the problem is that the organization and mandate of GATT go back to a time when environmental concerns were
irrelevant. Historically, interest in GATT has been restricted to corporations and trade associations—groups committed primarily to economic
growth, the maximizing of profit, and continued deregulation. Moreover,
trade negotiations have, for the most part, been conducted in secrecy. The
results of each round have come as a surprise to people concerned about
the environment.

The goals of GATT are clear: to reduce or eliminate as many import
restrictions as possible. However, reducing or eliminating import restrictions can undermine pollution control by making it easier for corporations
to relocate to areas where the cost of meeting environmental regulations is
lowest. This discourages fledgling environmental regulatory efforts in developing countries, which are scrambling for new investment, and it encourages countries to lower whatever environmental regulations they
might have put in place.[6]

By limiting the right of a country to restrict the export of vital resources and commodities, GATT indirectly removes important regulatory
tools that countries need to manage their resources effectively. GATT
negotiators want to eliminate all "nontariff trade barriers," which is another way of saying that they want to roll back or avoid environmental regulation. Numerous environmental initiatives in the United States and Europe
have already come under fire for this reason, although we have not yet seen
how conflicts between the mandates of GATT and the commitments incorporated into global environmental treaties will be resolved. One approach
may be to negotiate subsidiary agreements such as those proposed by
President Clinton as a way of increasing the acceptability of the North
American Free Trade Agreement (NAFTA). He has suggested that
NAFTA should not be ratified by the U.S. Congress until "side agreements" have been approved that would force Mexico to stiffen its environmental regulations and ensure their enforcement. This would keep American companies from crossing the Mexican border to escape the pollution
control regulations already in place in the United States.

The European Court has confronted cases like this, but the World
Court has not yet ruled on how the conflicting demands of free trade and
environmental protection should be handled. For example, in 1990 the
European Court found Denmark in breach of its obligations to the rest of
its trading partners in the European Economic Community (EEC) because
it adopted a waste reduction regulation requiring all beer and soft drinks
to be sold in returnable containers. To ensure that adequate systems were
in place to recover used containers effectively, only those approved by

Denmark's Environmental Protection Agency could be marketed. Other member states in the EEC objected, as did retail trade associations, which complained about the cost of establishing collection systems in Denmark. These groups argued for the right to market nonrefillable containers, including disposable beer cans. While acknowledging that no restraint of trade had actually occurred, the European Court concluded that the reuse regulations, requiring all marketers of containers to establish return systems, could be more expensive for importers than for domestic producers. In the end, the court found the Danish container legislation inconsistent with the principle of free trade.[7] This was prior to the signing of the Maastricht Treaty (which places environmental concerns on an even plane with development objectives within the European Community), but this kind of conflict is bound to occur again.

To avoid some of these problems in the future and to allow more opportunistic linkage between environment and trade, several GATT rules need to be amended. The long-term goal of the treaty should be to ensure that trade requirements are consistent with the goals of environmental treaties, and that opportunities for countries to expand trade are linked to their willingness to meet environmental treaty obligations. The Montreal Protocol, the CITES Convention, and the Basel Convention all indicate that trade sanctions are supposed to be used as enforcement tools. There is, however, no formal acknowledgment of this in the existing GATT agreement. Although the effectiveness of such sanctions will obviously depend on the overall economic capabilities of the countries involved (as well as the importance of the particular items to the economies in question), the appropriateness of such sanctions ought not to be in doubt. Right now, using trade sanctions in a discriminatory fashion is probably illegal.

The way to handle this kind of complexity is to be explicit in amending GATT, which may require a separate "green" round of GATT negotiations. The Organization of Economic Cooperation and Development (OECD)—which includes the twenty-four most industrialized nations in the world—is, in fact, preparing for such negotiations to reconcile the legal conflicts emerging between free (deregulated) trade agreements and international environmental regulations. These interrelationships require special attention.

## Linkage Guidelines

A crucial element in the success of a multilateral negotiation is the ability to add—very judiciously—issues and parties for purposes of expanding the zone of agreement. Negotiators should likewise be aware that subtracting issues and parties can be equally advantageous, particularly when an overstocked agenda creates management problems.

The appropriate scale and scope of a negotiation, and thus the use of issue linkage, depend on the size of the coalition required to respond to efforts to block consensus. Changes in the agenda must be made with the consent of all interested stakeholders. When there is unanimity, any linkage is acceptable. When doubts are raised, linkages must be argued "on their merits," that is, proponents must show either a functional or causal connection between issues or a past precedent legitimizing such a connection. Failing this, linkage is likely to be rejected. The key test of the acceptability of a proposed linkage is the impact it has on the long-term relationships among the parties.

Blackmail or threats of blackmail always destroy relationships. Even when a blackmailer is successful, a country's ill-gotten "victory" will, in all likelihood, lead to failure when it comes time to implement a treaty. Blackmail is one-sided extortion by means of threats. Linkage, on the other hand, must involve mutual advantage, voluntarily given, to be legitimate.

One of the ways in which small or less powerful parties can add to their bargaining strength is to build strategic alliances (that is, form blocking coalitions). For example, if the Group of Seventy-seven sticks together, it may be able to press its long-standing North-South agenda successfully. It will take increasingly talented management, by both convening bodies and secretariats, however, to handle the multilevel negotiations required to piece together a new global bargain while pursuing treaty-by-treaty discussions at the same time.

If there is an international commitment to work out a grand North-South bargain, of the sort described by Porter and Brown, it will undoubtedly take many years to complete. During that time, it would be prudent always to keep several treaties on the table at the same time, and to be open to nontraditional crossovers between separate policy arenas like environment and GATT. It would also be helpful to propose new ground rules, including amendments to GATT, spelling out the proper procedures for introducing issue linkage.[8]

# CHAPTER 6

# Monitoring and Enforcement in the Face of Sovereignty

Monitoring and enforcement provisions probably provide more opportunities for contention than any other single aspect of international treaty negotiation. In the environmental arena, the obvious reason for building monitoring provisions into global agreements is to catch and punish non-compliers. However, even if all parties to a treaty do everything required, the threat that prompted their treaty-making efforts might not be diminished. If the diagnosis of the problem, for instance, turned out to be wrong or the prescriptions were inadequate—because the scientists miscalculated, the politicians settled for too little, or the problem shifted in an important way—the results will be disappointing. Thus, there are other reasons for putting monitoring provisions into place, including learning more about the threat, determining how to adjust provisional standards and targets, and understanding how to build institutional capacity to respond more effectively.

Because mere enforcement will not necessarily produce the desired results, it is especially important to monitor in ways that enhance our understanding of the ecological systems involved and the actions that work to produce the results that the signatories seek. Monitoring for compliance focuses on gathering the information needed to punish noncompliance; monitoring for these other purposes requires the collection and analysis of different kinds of information.

## Technical and Legal Difficulties

Most monitoring arrangements in environmental treaties were created to reduce any country's ability to hide or profit from purposeful underperformance, but there is a host of technical and legal difficulties that plague all such efforts. A review of a meeting of experts designing a strategy for handling noncompliance with the Montreal Protocol illustrates some of these obstacles.[1] Representatives of twenty-nine countries and six international organizations attended this particular meeting, held in 1989 in Geneva. UNEP's acting chief of environmental law hosted the session, but the parties selected a representative from the United Kingdom, one of the signatories, to serve as chair. Because no uniform monitoring and enforcement provisions were available, the parties, as is usually the case, were forced to invent their own.

In his introductory statement, the chair of the working group emphasized that the issue of noncompliance "could be regarded as both large and small: large because noncompliance was an increasingly important topic and the Working Group's efforts were likely to set a precedent in the field of international law, and small because noncompliance was a single narrow issue within the Montreal Protocol."[2] He recommended that the meeting focus only on noncompliance problems specific to the Montreal Protocol.

Representatives from Venezuela and China were serving as vice chairs of the group, and a Swiss representative was elected rapporteur. (These individuals had never worked together before.) The group's discussions centered on written proposals submitted by the United States, the Netherlands, and Australia, as well as comments submitted ahead of time by Senegal, Spain, and Japan. They had only a few days to meet and just two sessions, several months apart, in which to prepare their recommendations.

The group reached a number of conclusions: (1) it was important to avoid drawing up an unnecessarily complex monitoring system; (2) the procedures used to deal with noncompliance should be nonconfrontational; (3) action under the noncompliance procedures should be initiated by parties registering their concerns with the secretariat; (4) both bilateral and collective responses would be appropriate; (5) the procedures proposed should not alter or weaken in any way the basic terms of the Vienna convention on which the protocol was based; (6) confidentiality had to be respected; (7) the secretariat's role should be that of an administrative, not a judicial, body; (8) the secretariat should compile all necessary data; (9) early indications of possible noncompliance should be resolved through administrative action by the secretariat or through diplomatic contacts between the parties; and (10) decisions about noncompliance should be taken only by a full meeting of the parties to the treaty.

The working group considered establishing a committee on noncompliance that could react quickly when complaints were filed. This provision was attractive to some participants because it would reduce the need for recourse to formal arbitration or to the International Court of Justice, but a majority of working group members were concerned that a committee on noncompliance would take on inappropriate judicial functions. Some members argued that such a committee was unnecessary because the secretariat could handle these tasks; moreover, the creation of a supranational body to review data was absolutely unacceptable. Others stated that they thought it was important to outline in advance specific actions that would be taken in response to noncompliance. Still other delegates made it clear they preferred not to be explicit; they wanted to leave all decisions to the discretion of a conference of the parties.

In the end, the working group concluded that a committee on noncompliance might be acceptable, but only if it worked on issues referred to it through the secretariat. They proposed a committee of five members elected by a meeting of the parties. The working group stressed that the committee should not perform any judicial or quasi-judicial functions. All decisions concerning responses to documented instances of noncompliance would have to be taken by the full meeting of the parties.

On the question of how new noncompliance rules should be adopted, most members favored using the already defined procedures for amending the terms of the Montreal Protocol. This would allow all parties subject to the new system to present their views, and the rules would become operational as soon as a vote was taken. Others were concerned about the possible implications for an outvoted minority, as well as the prospect of the noncompliance rules' taking on a mandatory quality. They preferred that the group make no specific recommendations. Finally, the working group discussed the possibility of adopting an additional conciliation procedure. Some members indicated they felt that this might be desirable, yet they did not think it should be a priority.

Several key conflicts can be identified in the interactions that took place at the 1989 meeting of experts. And, they are conflicts that seem to pervade all such efforts. First, efforts to design (let alone implement) procedures for monitoring compliance depend on the availability of believable data. The prospects for acquiring such information are highly constrained, particularly by the requirement that national sovereignty not be abridged. Sovereignty is as much a consideration in the design of monitoring arrangements (even those involving nothing more than periodic self-reporting) as it is in formulating sanctions or other responses to noncompliance. Because international law enshrines the right of sovereignty, all efforts to monitor performance, establish the accuracy of claims of noncompliance, punish proven noncompliers, or impose remedial action must be accepted voluntarily by the parties to a treaty. It is little wonder that the global environmental treaties signed thus far have such weak monitoring and enforcement provisions.

The Geneva meeting also illustrates how procedural issues become obstacles in developing effective monitoring provisions. Among the problems are the technical difficulties of verifying complaints of noncompliance; how to build the coalition necessary to put pressure on a noncomplier once documentation of a violation is obtained; and the difficulty of deciding who should have prosecutorial powers and responsibility for pursuing noncompliers. The monitoring and enforcement experiences associated with the CITES Convention and the Whaling Convention underscore still other monitoring difficulties.

Articles VIII and IX of the CITES Convention provide for monitoring and enforcement by the parties themselves. To become a party to the convention, a country must establish one or more competent management authorities to grant the special permits and certificates for the trade in wild flora and fauna provided for in the convention. In addition, a party must also establish an appropriate scientific body. Every signatory must submit annual reports concerning its implementation of the convention, using data gathered by its management and scientific authorities. Finally, the parties must agree to take measures to penalize trade and possession of controlled species and arrange for their return to the state of export.

Articles XI, XII, and XIII set out the role of the secretariat in monitoring and enforcing the provisions of the CITES Convention. The secretariat is supposed to "call the attention of the parties to the Convention" when appropriate and make recommendations regarding implementation. When the secretariat feels that the provisions of the convention are not being effectively implemented, it is empowered to "examine" the relevant information and make recommendations to the parties. The parties, however, are under no obligation to abide by the secretariat's recommendations. Each party has the right "to take a reservation" on any species listed in the various appendices to the convention. (Each appendix calls for a different level of protection). If a party takes a reservation, it is treated, with respect to that particular species, as a state that is not a party to the convention.

The secretariat publishes a report to the parties (based on data they have submitted) concerning alleged infractions. The report provides the parties with a record of instances in which it appears that significant violations have occurred. Although it describes attempts that have apparently been made to evade the provisions of the convention, it serves only as a cue to the parties to respond. Moreover, the secretariat's report covers only those cases in which the secretariat has been involved directly. Infractions dealt with directly by the parties are not covered in the secretariat's report.

The CITES Convention required the parties to establish a panel of experts to monitor and implement the downlisting of elephant populations on a case-by-case basis. A number of nongovernmental organizations, as well as affected states, provide nominees to serve on the panel. The panel's most important job is to suggest criteria for downlisting. These criteria are used to determine the status of elephant populations, the effectiveness of conservation measures, the adequacy of ivory-trade controls, the effectiveness of antipoaching measures, and whether the total level of animals taken, both legally and illegally, is sustainable.

The panel's recommendations, however, are only advisory to the parties. There is, in short, no method of authenticating any charge of noncompliance. The panel has an important role to play, but has no prosecutorial power; nor does the secretariat have that power. No one has responsibility for ensuring that documented noncompliance is remedied.

The International Convention for the Regulation of Whaling established the International Whaling Commission (IWC) to ensure proper and effective conservation and development of whale stocks. However, it gave the commission essentially no powers of enforcement. Article IX of the convention commits members of the commission to take appropriate measures to enforce the treaty and to punish violations by vessels and people under its jurisdiction, usually by fining them. Member countries are supposed to report all violations to the commission.

The IWC's system of self-enforcement has never worked to the satisfaction of any but the whaling nations. The convention does not describe when, where, or how to report violations (although the IWC has suggested reporting requirements). Each year, some infractions are reported, reasonable explanations for "errors" (and very occasionally punishment) are noted, and the offending parties are asked to prevent repeat occurrences.

In 1972 an international observer scheme was developed that placed observers from whaling nations on vessels of other whaling countries. These observers continue to be appointed by the IWC, based on nominations from all the whaling states. The observers have the right to monitor all installations and operations, but the standards they use are not widely circulated. Moreover, there is no mechanism for the IWC to respond to accusations of violations because these are all self-reported and therefore undisputed. A lack of a more independent monitoring capability has led, in the words of one longtime observer, to the "law of the least ambitious program."[3] That is, because restrictions can be imposed only by agreement of the whaling nations, collective action is limited to measures acceptable to the least enthusiastic party. The unofficial reports of nongovernmental organizations continue to suggest that there has only been partial reporting of treaty infractions.[4]

Thus far, the most effective means of getting compliance with IWC regulations has been through the imposition of unilateral economic sanctions, particularly by the United States. In 1970 the United States placed the eight largest species of whale on its endangered species list, banning imports of products derived therefrom. In 1972 the U.S. Marine Mammal Protection Act provided a legal framework for protecting the eight species (using a more comprehensive "ecosystem approach" that was quite different from the whale-by-whale "stock-assessment" approach, used by the IWC). In addition, other congressional action provided for a discretionary ban on the import of fisheries products from countries that "diminish the effectiveness of international fishing programs." Such countries are subject to a minimum fifty percent reduction of their permitted allocation of fish harvested inside U.S. territorial waters. Action of this sort has proven to be an effective tool, although the United States used this threat to persuade Japan to agree to a zero quota on commercial catches but did not use the thrust to push for remedial action in instances in which treaty infractions have been documented.

"Outsiders" do not have standing to sue nations charged with violating the Whaling Convention. Indeed, there has not been a single case of noncompliance brought before the International Court of Justice. Nations that believe whales are being mismanaged have had no choice but to be supportive of the conservation efforts of the IWC. In one sense, this has been helpful because it has bolstered the IWC's role as a meaningful regulatory forum. However, whaling nations dissatisfied with the IWC's efforts have the power to withdraw. Indeed, they can, at any time, establish a separate organization to regulate whaling, and they have often threatened to do so. Although unilateral action by the United States has, in the past, been effective in pressing countries to accept quotas they would otherwise have rejected, Norway recently announced its intention to resume commercial whaling in spite of the zero quota imposed by the IWC.

Most treaties rely on self-reporting. If a country refuses to submit the required reports, or resists independent efforts to validate the accuracy of reports, enforcement is stymied. Without independent monitoring data, it may be impossible to prove that the charges made by one country (or NGO) against another are accurate. Indeed, without documented evidence of wrongdoing, it is enormously difficult to build a coalition strong enough to force a noncomplying nation to change its behavior.

In addition to the need to catch and punish noncompliers, or free riders, there are frequently overshadowed but still very important reasons for strengthening global environmental monitoring arrangements. For example, it is important to find out whether countries are, in fact, capable of collecting the information required by a treaty or of completing the requisite analysis of the data in a timely fashion. Documentation of difficulties along these lines can ensure that adequate technical assistance or training are provided to countries that need them.

All kinds of treaty-tightening mechanisms, such as the "racheting" procedure included in the Montreal Protocol or the "relief valve" proposed for inclusion in a climate change protocol (that is, allowing for targets or timetables to be adjusted if it turns out to be more expensive to stabilize greenhouse gas emissions than the parties expected), depend on reliable monitoring. The problem is that signatory countries will not only try to cover up instances of noncompliance but also seek to hide their monitoring inadequacies. They do this to avoid attracting attention. Admitting their inabilities might trigger investigations by outside technical experts, which, in turn, could turn up unexpected violations. The fact that monitoring reports might also lead to significant revisions in unreasonable requirements or encourage the allocation of additional technical assistance or financial support have not been sufficient reasons to encourage cooperation.

Sometimes national monitoring reports can be double-checked by using satellites, but the use of remote-sensing data has also been challenged as an infringement on national sovereignty. Unless suspected violations can be verified in a way that does not violate prevailing notions of sovereignty, noncompliance cannot be addressed. Gathering the necessary proof in the face of such resistance has been almost impossible.

The Montreal Protocol working group on noncompliance went to great lengths to keep the secretariat out of any independent fact-finding or adjudicatory role. The CITES and Whaling conventions also restricted their secretariats to relatively passive assignments. If the prosecutorial responsibilities of the secretariat are restricted, who, then, is supposed to pursue the appropriate investigations or negotiate remedial actions with those charged with infractions? When the signatories to a treaty number more than a hundred, and a conference of the parties involves several thousand delegates, it is unlikely that an effective discussion, let alone thoughtful action, will result. In the final analysis, all the burden is on individual countries to initiate bilateral talks aimed at getting noncompliers to take remedial steps. Unfortunately, there will not always be a powerful country in a position to take this responsibility. Moreover, it is not clear, how any single country will find the data needed to pursue noncompliers, or that, given the state of North-South relations, the rest of the world wants large economic powers to play such a policing role.

In addition to the problems cited thus far, there are still other difficulties that affect particular treaties because of their context—for example, those associated with measuring emissions and resource utilization levels.

These involve primarily technical and economic, not political, issues, but they must be resolved. Some scientists and engineers have argued that it would not be difficult to put the right monitoring devices in all the right locations to track the performance of most countries pursuant to most environmental treaties. The problem, though, is ensuring that these devices work properly. Moreover, the cost of building such systems would be enormous.

Furthermore, merely tracking the behavior of signatory nations is not enough. Changes in background, or what are called "ambient," conditions must also be assessed regularly to ensure that other (natural and human) forces are not working at cross-purposes to the efforts of the signatories. The most important question is not whether the signatories are behaving but whether the objectives of the treaty are being met. Regular monitoring of the ocean-dumping activities of the signatories to the London Dumping Convention, for example, is not sufficient to evaluate the effectiveness of that treaty. The overall state of ocean water quality and aquatic life must be assessed on a continuing and comprehensive basis as well. Broader monitoring of this type was part of the original idea behind UNEP's Global Environmental Monitoring System (GEMS), but it has not been possible to achieve anything approaching this level of data collection. Systematic monitoring of this sort would not only transcend the United Nations' financial capacity, but far exceed the political mandate that UNEP has been given.

Finally, even if the most elaborate monitoring systems were operating effectively, this would not necessarily clarify the actions that should be taken once damage is found. Nor would perfect monitoring data oblige or enable noncomplying countries to reverse the adverse effects they had caused. If, for example, a country had clearly allowed an area to become contaminated with toxic wastes—in violation of the Basel Convention—it might not necessarily have the skills, technology, or money to effectuate a cleanup. The United States, for instance, has spent more than $15 billion and thirteen years trying to clean up several hundred contaminated Superfund sites, only to discover that it does not have the knowledge or the will required to complete the task. What does this say about the chances that poorer countries would be able to respond effectively when damage is discovered?

Given this array of obstacles, it may be hard to understand why anyone even bothers to include monitoring and enforcement provisions in global environmental treaties. The answer, surprisingly, is that most countries comply most of the time with most of the treaties they sign. Just why this is true is the source of some theoretical debate.

# A Theory of Compliance

Much of the debate about how best to bring about compliance with international treaties revolves around the advantages and disadvantages of direct techniques for deterring noncompliance versus indirect techniques for encouraging adherence to the rules. Most international relations experts believe that countries will inevitably act in their own self-interest, and that enlightened self-interest encompasses an awareness that every nation is part of the web of international economic and political relationships. Violating the norms and commitments central to these relationships will inevitably lead to isolation or, worse still, expulsion from the club of nations. All countries understand, therefore, that their best interests are almost always served by living up to their treaty obligations.

At the same time, many elected leaders and environmental activists believe that more must be done to expand the scope of international law to diminish the importance of sovereignty and enhance the enforcement powers of global authorities. The 1989 Hague Declaration calling for a new worldwide legislative body with enforcement powers was the most far-reaching attempt to strengthen international authority over global environmental matters. The conference at the Hague involved twenty-four nations. It was proposed by France and organized with the help of the Netherlands and Norway. The major political and economic powers, however—the United States, the former Soviet Union, China, and Britain—all failed to attend the meeting.

The Hague Declaration called for the development of new principles of international law "including new and more effective decision-making and enforcement mechanisms." It called also for an expansion of the institutional authority of the United Nations. Most important, it proposed that unanimity would no longer be required to make binding decisions, and that the International Court of Justice would have jurisdiction over compliance with UN-sponsored treaties. Three dozen countries signed the declaration, yet it seems to have faded from view, receiving almost no attention at the 1992 Earth Summit.

Those who signed the declaration were heads of state, indicating an apparent willingness to see sovereignty diminished, at least under some circumstances, and to submit to "nonunanimous decisions of supranational entities for the good of the world community."[5] Other proposals to expand the scope of international law governing the enforcement of global environmental treaties would go even further. Edith Brown Weiss, former associate general counsel at the U.S. Environmental Protection Agency, has proposed a "Declaration of Planetary Rights and Obligations to Future

Generations" that would lay out principles of intergenerational equity. Similarly, Jacques-Yves Cousteau has gathered more than four million petition signatures (and is seeking six million more) in support of a five-point "Bill of Rights for Future Generations" that he wants the UN General Assembly to adopt.

The five principles in the Cousteau "Bill of Rights" are (1) future generations have a right to an uncontaminated and undamaged Earth and to its enjoyment as the source of human history, of culture, and of social bonds that make each generation and individual a member of one human family; (2) each generation, sharing in the estate and heritage of the Earth, has a duty as trustee for future generations to prevent irreversible and irreparable harm to life on Earth and to human freedom and dignity; (3) it is, therefore, the paramount responsibility of each generation to maintain a constantly vigilant and prudential assessment of technological disturbances and modifications adversely affecting life on Earth, the balance of nature, and the evolution of mankind in order to protect the rights of future generations; (4) all appropriate measures, including education, research, and legislation, shall be taken to guarantee these rights and to ensure that they not be sacrificed for present expedience and convenience; and (5) governments, nongovernmental organizations, and individuals are urged, therefore, to implement these principles imaginatively, as if in the very presence of those future generations whose rights we seek to establish and perpetuate. If such principles were to become part of the body of written international law, presumably they would be enforceable through the World Court. More important, environmental groups within each country could use the declaration to justify their demands for stronger domestic environmental legislation.

Alexander Timoshenko, a specialist in international law from the former Soviet Union, has argued that the concept of "ecological security" should also be added to the body of international law. This would acknowledge that environmental protection is a condition for human survival and make the world community as a whole responsible for ensuring it. This harks back to the plea of the Stockholm Conference on the Human Environment that the "heritage of mankind" be given legal recognition and that nongovernmental organizations be empowered to challenge the right of national governments to violate that heritage. Under Timoshenko's proposal, states would be obligated to prevent "serious harmful anthropogenic impacts on the Earth." He has urged that a precise, juridically explicit formulation of the principle of ecological responsibility (at a minimum, regarding termination of harmful activities and compensation for damage) be included in an international "Code of Ecological Security."[6]

Weiss, Cousteau, Timoshenko, and most of the signers of the Hague

Declaration want to embody in international law a set of global resource-management principles and obligations that will empower multilateral organizations, nongovernmental organizations, and the World Court to supersede the fundamental right of sovereign nations to have the final say over the decisions that directly affect them. If such new law were to come into effect, countries would be under increasing pressure to meet existing treaty requirements, submit to independent reviews of their monitoring reports, and adhere to the mandates of all international environmental treaties. This would not obviate the problems of enforcement, though, because it begs the question of how the United Nations or any other international agency will deter noncompliance with these or any other principles.

The fierce protection of national sovereignty is unlikely to erode. Instead, it makes more sense to seek what Abram and Antonia Chayes call "compliance without enforcement."[7] Monitoring that is not primarily keyed to compliance, and enforcement that does not depend on the imposition of sanctions or reprisals are much more likely to be acceptable. Indirect mechanisms that induce compliance but do not hinge on the rewriting of international law are more likely to produce results quickly and reliably.

In his book, *Improving Compliance With International Law* (1981), Roger Fisher distinguishes between the internal factors that cause countries to respect standing rules, and the factors that cause them to change their behavior once they have been caught out of compliance. Fisher attributes first-order compliance (respect for standing rules) to enlightened self-interest and the perceived fairness of the procedures used to derive the rules. He does not dismiss the threat of force or punishment as unimportant but downplays it. Fisher attributes second-order compliance (a willingness to change inappropriate behavior) to the legitimacy of the methods used to substantiate charges of noncompliance, the blending of international requirements into domestic law, the general acceptability of international institutions, the prior establishment of precise rules about remedies, and the capacity of enforcement agencies to apply sanctions effectively. Several of these factors could be exploited to a far greater extent than they have been in achieving compliance with global environmental treaties.

As Chayes and Chayes point out, Chapter VII of the UN Charter provides for compulsory economic or military sanctions by the Security Council, like these imposed in 1990 following Iraq's attack on Kuwait. Such measures, however, have been employed only four times since 1945. Moreover, as Chayes and Chayes found in their extensive study of treaty making, such sanctions have never been used to secure treaty compliance. When they were used, it was to punish "pariah states" that had behaved unacceptably in the eyes of a broad segment of the international community. There is not a single instance of a secretariat for a global environmental treaty winning Security Council approval for an embargo, blockade, or armed intervention in response to even repeated violations of environmental treaties. Furthermore, expulsion from the treaty regime, which Chayes and Chayes argue is characteristically used as a penalty against those who fail to meet treaty obligations, is self-defeating; it only makes it harder for the remaining parties to achieve their environmental objectives.

It is possible that the *threat* of formal sanctions has a deterrent effect, yet even this is not firmly established. Deterrence theory, as explained by Thomas Schelling and others, requires that a threat have credibility.[8] Given the experience of the past several decades, especially as it relates to noncompliance with global environmental treaties, such credibility would be hard to muster. So, even if the scope of international law is expanded and nongovernmental organizations are given standing to sue noncompliers in the World Court, it is not clear who would apply the requisite sanctions. It seems more important, then, to learn how to use the indirect factors that induce countries to see it in their self-interest to comply.

Jane Mansbridge, in her book *Beyond Self-Interest* (1992), suggests that self-interest is often too narrowly construed as selfishness. Mansbridge and her colleagues demonstrate that social stability has always been grounded in "cooperation and consensus, and not merely in exchange or conflict." Nations accept and adhere to treaty requirements much of the time because they are convinced by principled arguments, respect the evidence that others have provided, and share a sense of responsibility for "the common good." Whether we want to call this altruism or view it as another way of defining self-interest, it helps to explain why countries do things that hurt them in the short-run but help them (and others) in the long run.

Another important piece of the theoretical puzzle is explained by Robert Alexrod in *The Evolution of Cooperation* (1987). He and other game theorists have demonstrated that relationships between competitive actors will, over time, tend toward cooperation as each realizes that the benefits of a mutually supportive relationship outweigh the possible short-term advantages of selfishness. Elinor Ostrom has extended this insight into the realm of shared environmental resources. In *Managing the Common* (1991), she shows quite conclusively why and how communities work out equitable ways of sharing both the benefits and costs of maintaining "common pool resources," even without the intervention of a strong central authority. The so-called tragedy of the commons, then, that has for so long ruled out thinking about why countries are likely to defect from multilateral agreements when it serves their short-term interests, turns out not necessarily to be a good basis for predicting whether countries will comply with global environmental treaties. They cannot be expected only to comply most of the time, but, if Ostrom is right, they will even take the initiative to work out cooperative arrangements because short-term economic considerations are not as important to them as long-term stability and political reciprocity.

In addition to enlightened self-interest, there are several other non-coercive factors that account for voluntary compliance. These include financial incentives, linked policy commitments, and promises of future considerations. In general, the limiting feature of such indirect measures, as Chayes and Chayes point out, is that they must be financed and managed, usually by other members of the relevant regime because no international organization has the taxing power to raise money or the political authority to spend it. And, securing promised contributions is difficult, especially in recessionary times. (The United States, for example, increasingly eager to use the United Nations in its war against Iraq, is more than $800 million in arrears in payment of its United Nations dues.)

The creation of the new, multipurpose Global Environmental Facility, or GEF, may signal a way to overcome some of these problems and make it easier to use financial incentives to encourage compliance. The GEF began in 1990 as a three-year experiment, but it may well become permanent. It was initially proposed by France as a means of funneling money and technological assistance to developing countries to help them cope with climate change caused by the emission of greenhouse gases, pollution of international waters (caused by spills and the accumulation of wastes), destruction of biological diversity through the degradation of natural habitats, and depletion of stratospheric ozone.

The GEF's initial operating budget goal was $1.3 billion: $800 million in a core trust fund, $300 million for grant making on highly concessionary terms, and $200 million provided under the terms of the Montreal Protocol to help developing countries comply with the mandate to phase out ozone-destroying substances. Twenty-four countries (nine of them in the developing world) pledged the $800 million for the core fund prior to 1992. Substantial additional funding was promised at the Earth Summit—approximately $2 billion more a year for the next several years—by Japan, Germany, France, the United States, Britain, and Canada, although it is hard to know exactly what portion of this money represents additional commitments (over and above "regular" foreign aid). It is also not clear how much of this money will be administered through the GEF and how much will come through other bilateral aid channels. The creation of a standing fund will make it easier to offer credible financial incentives as a reward for compliance in future environmental treaty negotiationss. The availability of these funds will not depend on the willingness of the next set of treaty negotiators to make good on their promises. Although the amount pledged at the Earth Summit was far short of the $125 billion a year that the UNCED secretary-general indicated would be needed to implement Agenda 21, it does represent a move toward creation of a permanent fund to help ensure the effective implementation of global environmental agreements.

The United States insisted that the creation of the $200 million fund to help developing nations implement the terms of the Montreal Protocol would not set a precedent. China, India, and other Group of Seventy-seven members had indicated that without additional financial help and a promise of access to new technologies they would not sign the Montreal Protocol. (India has still not signed, even though the fund was created.) Yet, the creation of the GEF appears to have set just the sort of precedent the Americans wanted to avoid. Pledges of billions of additional dollars for as yet unspecified purposes in the developing world, whether restricted in some way to implementing existing conventions or not, indicates a greater willingness to use financial incentives rather than threats to encourage countries to sign treaties and to make compliance more likely.

Compliance is further complicated when disputes emerge. If a country stands by the accuracy of its monitoring reports, refutes the legitimacy of contradictory monitoring information from independent sources, or disagrees with how treaty provisions ought to be interpreted, this makes enforcement trickier—whether direct or indirect mechanisms are employed. It is important, therefore, that a dispute resolution process, acceptable to all the parties, is included as part of every treaty. A functioning regime needs both ways of settling controversies among the parties as well as ways of resolving questions of treaty interpretation. As Roger Fisher points out, whether a dispute is a consequence of alleged noncompliance or whether alleged noncompliance is a consequence of a dispute is not especially important; they go hand in hand.

It is somewhat surprising how little effort has gone into designing more effective dispute resolution systems to include in global environmental treaties. Article 14 of the Climate Change Convention signed at the Earth Summit covering "settlement of disputes" is only a single page long. It basically says that parties in dispute should seek to settle their differences through negotiation or some other peaceful means of their own choosing. When ratifying, accepting, approving, or acceding to the convention, or at any time thereafter, a party can note a disagreement and ask that it be addressed by the International Court of Justice or arbitrated in accordance with procedures adopted in the future by the conference of the parties. Prior to that, at the request of any party, a conciliation commission is supposed to be created (with an equal number of members appointed by each party concerned and a chair chosen jointly by the members appointed by each party) to help work out disputes.

There is no mention of possible mediation by the secretariat, UNEP, or any other neutral party chosen by the secretariat or by the World Court. No use of minitrials, ad hoc scientific panels, or other hybrid forms of dispute settlement is suggested. Given that compliance is, in part, a function of each party's sense that it has been treated fairly, it would make sense to devote more effort to inventing additional dispute handling systems—appropriate to global environmental treaties—that would increase the parties' sense that their concerns were being addressed. In the absence of effective dispute handling procedures, countries often feel justified in letting their treaty commitments lapse.[9]

In summary, compliance with global environmental treaties, according to the theorists, rests on either enforcement by an international police force strong enough to impose the law or indirect strategies for inducing appropriate governmental behavior. Given the prominence of the principle of sovereignty, and the unwillingness of the United Nations to use force to achieve treaty compliance, it is important to do more to convince each nation that its self-interest is best served by complying with all treaties it has signed. Countries will have an easier time accepting such an assertion if they receive financial help and feel they are being treated fairly when disputes arise.

## Getting Around the Sovereignty Problem

Oran Young argues that the prospect of "shaming"—exposing treaty violations to the public—may be a source of even greater fear than the application of sanctions. "Policymakers," he writes, "like private individuals are sensitive to the social opprobrium that accompanies violations of widely accepted behavioral prescriptions."[10] These feelings, Chayes and Chayes point out, are intensified by having to confront colleagues demanding explanations for violations. This, of course, explains the resistance, described earlier, that countries sometimes display toward reporting requirements, independent reviews of national reports, or other mechanisms designed to inform the public of their behavior. Monitoring is effective, then, because it increases "transparency," although because anything other than pure self-reporting typically runs afoul of claims of sovereignty, this is not easy to achieve.

Although countries insist that no one outside their borders ought to be empowered to second-guess them, the sovereignty argument does not apply to people and organizations within their own borders. Thus, one way around the sovereignty problem is to create groups within each country to take responsibility for monitoring compliance. These groups, especially when they join forces on a worldwide basis, may be able to shame noncomplying nations into changing their behavior. By working together, highly motivated local activists can achieve the competence and credibility they need to bring the full weight of international opinion to bear on noncompliers. We have seen this model before; it is the approach that Amnesty International uses in pursuing noncompliance with the United Nations' human rights provisions.

To build a parallel monitoring and enforcement system in the environmental field, all UN member states would have to sign a protocol equivalent to the Optional Protocol to the International Convenant on Civil and Political Rights. Countries that signed this agreement would be permitting their citizens to pursue individual complaints against violators of global environmental treaties. A UN environmental violations committee (perhaps with the same number of members, eighteen, as the UN Human Rights Committee) would adjudicate all complaints. A working group on noncompliance would receive information from what might be called the "Green Amnesty International" (GAI) as well as other nongovernmental organizations.

The United Nations has three procedures for publicizing human rights abuses by governments; all involve increased transparency. Parallels for pursuing environmental treaty violations would need to be created. The first, equivalent to the United Nation's Economic and Social Council (ECOSOC) Resolution 728F, would create an environmental violations committee, give it authority to receive communications concerning treaty violations, and empower it to send notices of alleged violations to the governments involved. Under a mechanism similar to the one established by ECOSOC Resolution 1235, allegations of violations could then be the subject of public discussion in the United Nations. Finally, under an equivalent of ECOSOC Resolution 1503, the United Nations would set up the necessary administrative machinery to ensure that communications from individuals could be assessed in closed session to determine whether there were deliberate violations. Such confidential reviews would culminate in an announcement by the chair of the environmental violations committee of a list of offenders.

How would "Green Amnesty International," the league of nongovernmental organizations, be organized?[11] If it followed the Amnesty International model, the organization's stated objective would be to work for prompt and fair resolution of environmental treaty violations under internationally recognized norms. To the extent that something like the Brundtland Commission's Declaration of the Right to Nature Conservation, Environmental Protection, and Sustainable Development (see Appendix B) was adopted, it would be clear what these norms were. In the absence of a single codified statement of principles, GAI would have to depend on the preambles of all the global environmental treaties for these norms.

GAI would call upon governments to comply with all environmental treaties. Such requests would be made through GAI members or branches around the world. Individual GAI members would be asked, by the GAI international secretariat, to register complaints about possible treaty violations. GAI would also issue case-by-case advisories to its members suggesting which remedies to request. GAI would, if necessary, send observers to selected environmental sites believed to be at risk.

The GAI secretariat would work closely with other international nongovernmental organizations, taking advantage of the three types of communication procedures available through the UN Environmental Violations Committee. It might also push the secretariats or the members of individual treaty regimes to act, or seek intervention by the UN secretary-general or one of the other arms of the United Nations like UNEP, UNDP, the GEF, or the World Bank whenever treaty violations were alleged.

Research would be central to GAI's efforts. The research department of the international secretariat would collect and analyze information about violations of environmental treaties. With information coming in from many sources, GAI would have to check all claims carefully before any action could be taken. Accuracy and impartiality would be crucial to maintaining the organization's reputation.

GAI's purpose would not be to condemn governments or individual leaders but, rather, to push for corrective action. Its research would be focused exclusively on environmental violations, irrespective of political considerations. To help guard against political bias, staff in the international secretariat would not be allowed to work on investigations in their own countries. GAI would also be used as a resource by scholars, journalists, and others seeking information on the status of treaty compliance.

Research would be only the first step. Charges would have to be verified by independent observers in the field. Suggestions for action would be sent out by the secretariat to GAI's worldwide network of members, groups, and supporters. The secretariat would rely on teams of area specialists for advice on what to recommend. Researchers would prepare background summaries, as well as strategy and briefing papers on which GAI's publicity efforts and diplomatic initiatives would be based. The secretariat could also draw on an international board of scientific advisers.

Every month the international secretariat would choose a few cases of environmental treaty violations, each identified by a GAI branch. The details of each case would be described in GAI's newsletter and sent to all members and subscribers for immediate attention. Drafts of appropriate letters would be included to send to public officials and the press. Members could send appeals to the relevant embassies in their own countries that would be forwarded to the relevant authorities. GAI branches and members could also encourage their local media to publish these letters.

Every year, based on its studies of noncompliance patterns, GAI would select several countries for particular attention. Members in these countries would conduct special publicity campaigns in behalf of environmental protection and sustainable development. GAI missions might be sent to observe sites of marked concern in these countries. Site visit reports would be prepared and submitted to the government involved, before publication.

GAI would seek to be represented at the United Nations through offices in New York, Geneva, Vienna, and also at UNESCO in Paris. It would seek consultative status with ECOSOC so it would have a place on various ECOSOC committees. It would also send representatives to all UNEP meetings. It might have section offices in Strasbourg (for the Council on Europe), Brussels (for the EC), New York (for the Organization of American States), Nairobi (for African nations), and Bangkok (for Asian countries).

Within a few years, GAI—like Amnesty International, on which it is modeled—could have as many as 350,000 members, subscribers, and supporters in more than 170 countries and territories. Membership would be open to anyone who supported the goals of the organization. Most GAI activists would probably belong to local environmental organizations as well, but in some sections of the world this would not be the case.

GAI's active members would work together in groups. These local groups would be the basic building block of the organization. GAI—again, based on Amnesty's experience—could aim to have as many as 2,500 local branches in more than fifty countries registered with the international secretariat. Most branches might have approximately ten to fifteen active members, but some would have many more. Each branch would be responsible for raising the funds needed to cover its own operating expenses. All local groups would be free to organize themselves as they liked, but they would be obligated to observe the general guidelines issued by the international secretariat. Local groups would receive weekly mailings from the secretariat that would include campaign materials, requests for action, country reports, and general educational materials on environmental treaty making.

The essence of the GAI approach would be to shame noncomplying countries into changing their behavior. Through a combination of careful in-country documentation of instances of noncompliance, publicity, and the weight of world opinion, an international league of nongovernmental organizations could help to expand the scope of global monitoring beyond anything currently prescribed in an environmental treaty. In addition to monitoring compliance, such NGO involvement could also help to spot situations in which additional technical assistance is required (even if the countries themselves have not requested it). GAI reports would play a role in treaty tightening, and all of this would be done without any further encroachment on national sovereignty than has already occurred in the human rights field.

## Nearly Self-Enforcing Agreements

One other indirect means of increasing compliance with global environmental accords is to structure written treaties differently. In both domestic and international contexts it has been possible, from time to time, to design nearly self-enforcing agreements.[12] That is, by including appropriate contract provisions, the need for either surveillance or police power has been dramatically reduced. Through the posting of bonds, for example, paid back upon performance or sacrificed in the case of non-performance, those who have promised to live up to their environmental protection responsibilities have been given an added incentive to do so. The requirement of insurance policies or the equivalent has made it possible to guarantee that some environmental quality objectives will be met without the need for litigation or the use of force. There are numerous opportunities to apply concepts like these in global environmental treaty making.

The easiest and most effective device for ensuring compliance is the requirement that parties to a contract—or in the case of global environmental agreements, potential signatories to a treaty—post a bond. This money is held by a reliable neutral party. As long as the signatories live up to their obligations, the bond accumulates interest that is ultimately returned. If, however, a party violates the agreement, some or all of the bond it posted would be sacrificed. In the case of global environmental treaties, perhaps countries that comply for a period of ten years might get all the interest back on their bonds.

The size of the bond required would be keyed to either the nature of the risks associated with noncompliance or a country's ability to pay. Bonds that are sacrificed could be used to underwrite the cost of UN-sponsored environmental monitoring. Bonds could also work the other way: for every year a party complies with a treaty, it might recoup a predetermined portion of its bond. All debits or payouts, though, and the basis for making them, would have to be specified quite carefully ahead of time, and an arbiter acceptable to all sides would have to be named to help resolve disputes.

Liquidating bonds (that is those that return money as promised performance is completed) are frequently used at the municipal level in the United States to make sure that developers build the roads, pave the streets, put in the streetlights, and do the other things they have agreed to do when they are given permission to build houses. Many municipalities require bonds equal to the cost of the improvements that have been promised. A portion of the bond is returned as the work is completed.

In the international treaty-making arena, it would be more difficult to calculate the level at which bonds should be set. It would also be hard to know exactly which yardstick of performance to use in determining how much money should be returned each year because global environmental treaties are meant to continue indefinitely. Nevertheless, even the posting of a symbolic bond, returnable after just a few years, might serve several valuable purposes. A country would be more likely to enact domestic legislation and regulations encouraging its citizens to comply in order to get its money back. Even after the bonds are returned, the importance of complying with the terms of the treaty would have been conveyed to all citizens. Moreover, it is highly unlikely a country would repeal the relevant laws after it has recouped its bond. Failure to comply would add to the resources the relevant treaty secretariat can use to remedy some of the adverse impacts of noncompliance. Finally, it would be easier to hold the behavior of a noncomplying party up to public scrutiny because "guilt" would not have to be established through lengthy (and often ineffective) legal proceedings but, rather, would be inherent in the sacrifice of the bond.

Another device, sometimes used in international business dealings to achieve nearly self-enforcing agreements, is the requirement that a party purchase an insurance policy. This holds its "partners" harmless in case of noncompliance. So, for instance, if a corporation wanted to build a factory in a foreign country but was worried that the country might change its laws or appropriate the factory once the plant was built (but before sufficient profits were realized to cover the capital outlay), the corporation could ask the country involved to take out an insurance policy naming the factory owner as beneficiary. Once the factory owner had realized sufficient profit (or received promised subsidies), the policy would be allowed to lapse.

Although the insurance idea may not be immediately analogous to the world of global environmental treaty making, there may be some applications. For example, all signatories to a treaty might be required to buy insurance (instead of posting bonds) designed to hold the rest of the world harmless should that country fail to live up to its treaty obligations. Such an insurance policy might be expensive for countries that had reneged on their promises in previous years, but it would discourage bad behavior. For countries with good records, however, policies would become increasingly less expensive, dropping in price each year for as long as the country remained in compliance. Perhaps the GEF or the United Nations could be made the beneficiary of such insurance policies. The point, of course, is not to raise money but to encourage strict compliance without the need for an international police force.

Still another device that has been included in written contracts to encourage self-enforcement is a detailed schedule of required performance. The notion is that the parties would be asked to take only one small step at a time in the direction they have promised to go. Each subsequent step would be conditioned on all the other signatories having done what they had promised to do. In this way, no country would feel that it was being asked to make sacrifices while others reaped the advantages of noncompliance. In domestic contracts between environmental groups and development companies, for example, agreements have been devised that require each "side" to take a series of small steps as others complete the tasks they had promised to undertake. So, for instance, environmental groups have promised not to oppose development permit requests publicly as long as the developer completes promised site improvements. Neither is asked to make a blanket promise; rather, they have agreed to follow a schedule whereby compliance by one is conditioned on continued compliance by the other, until both complete all their obligations.

In the global treaty-making setting, this might take the form of annual reviews of compliance leading to suspension of the treaty unless every signatory has done what it promised. This might, at first blush, appear to play into the hands of noncompliers, but such a process, if it leads to a more serious effort to comply, would actually end up producing stronger agreements. No country would be eager to be the one that caused suspension of all international efforts to combat a global risk.

It may not be possible to find ways of making global environmental treaties entirely self-enforcing, but moves in this direction make sense. The key to working out such agreements is the precise penalty or payout that countries are asked to sign on to at the time they ratify a global agreement. This makes the political benefits of being a party to a treaty regime available only to those who post the required bonds, produce the required insurance policy, or agree to let others off the hook if they do not comply later on. Because there are clearly short-term political benefits that accrue to signing global environmental treaties (as those heads of state at the Earth Summit realized when they were applauded at home for signing the Biodiversity Convention and the Climate Change Convention), these are not unimportant considerations.

## Do We Need the Green Police?

There have been proposals to create a strong international-treaty-enforcement entity—or what I call the "green police." However, if we need an international police force to ensure compliance with global environmental treaties, we have failed to formulate agreements properly. The GAI would not be a police force. There are parts of the world, particularly in Latin America, where the military is eager to take on additional environmental enforcement responsibilities (for example, patroling the rain forest to prevent unauthorized burning of land), but the UN peacekeeping forces (also known as the "blue helmets") are not looking for such an assignment. Moreover, it is unlikely that a "green police" force of sufficient size could be pieced together on a volunteer basis. It is also unlikely that the Security Council would authorize the use of UN forces to pursue compliance with environmental treaties.

Thus, if the threat of force is the only effective deterrent, and only deterrence or other direct measures are sufficiently powerful to produce compliance, then environmental treaty making is probably doomed. But, if indirect measures can encourage countries to define their self-interest in ways that produce compliance—without the threat of force—then the chances of successfully implementing these treaties is much greater. To the extent that compliance generates financial benefits, countries will make more of an effort to ensure that their citizens take these treaty requirements seriously.

Extensive monitoring of each signatory's compliance with the terms of all global environmental treaties is important, not just to ensure that no one gains an advantage through nonperformance but also because monitoring is the key to understanding the threats that motivated collective action in the first place and to successfully recalibrating the standards and timetables contained in each treaty. Continued improvement in treaty making depends on learning as much as possible about the ability of the parties to meet their obligations, and about the relative effectiveness of different strategies for managing or reducing environmental risks.

The creation of a worldwide league of nongovernmental organizations—like a "Green Environmental Amnesty"—could substantially improve the prospects for effective monitoring. No country is eager to be publicly exposed as a "cheater," so by ensuring greater transparency in the reporting of national performance, the odds of getting accurate self-reports will go up. This might well lead to more effective long-term administration of environmental treaties.

Although it seems to be true that most countries comply most of the time with most of the treaties they sign, this leaves lots of room for half-hearted compliance or inadvertent noncompliance. We also have very little sense of what the actual track record on compliance with environmental treaties has been.[13] Global environmental monitoring efforts have been haphazard, and because of concerns about sovereignty, the United Nations has been almost entirely dependent on self-reporting. Even if the principle of sovereignty survives current efforts to reduce its scope through the rewriting of international law, there are ways of ensuring greater compliance and more effective treaty implementation that have not yet been tried.

# CHAPTER 7

# Reforming the System: The Salzburg Initiative and Other Proposals for Change

In the fall of 1989, with support from the Massachusetts-based Dana Greeley Foundation for Peace and Justice, a small group of scholars, diplomats, and environmental activists met at the Program on Negotiation at Harvard Law School. Their goal was to explore possible institutional reforms that might encourage more effective global environmental treaty making in the face of growing mistrust among nations, continued governmental unwillingness to acknowledge mounting evidence of new environmental threats, and the unremitting desire on the part of most nations to protect their sovereignty. The group identified several factors that seemed to account for past collective action on the environment: the existence of the scientific equivalent of a "smoking gun" (for example, a hole in the ozone layer), strong worldwide pressure from activists and the news media acknowledging a threat, and the emergence of a simply stated action that might address the problem or reduce the risk (for example, phase out the production of CFCs).

The team translated its findings into a set of propositions and presented them to Maurice Strong, secretary-general for the UN Conference on Environment and Development. When he urged the team to continue its explorations, it created a secretariat at the MIT-Harvard Public Disputes Program at Harvard Law School.

In mid-1990, with the help of Bradford Morse, then president of the Salzburg Seminar (in Salzburg, Austria), the team convened a much larger international assembly of diplomats, scientists, negotiation experts, international relations theorists, development specialists, and environmental activists. The discussions at the Salzburg meeting were characterized by energetic exchanges among attendees from the North and South (as well as those from East and West). As the talks progressed and the focus shifted from an analysis of specific global environmental threats to an examination of the larger treaty-making system, there was clear agreement: the treaty-making system could indeed be strengthened. The outcome of these deliberations took the form of the Salzburg Initiative, a ten-point agenda for reforming the global environmental treaty-making process.[1]

The group put this package of reforms before as many world leaders as possible, and urged the UNCED secretariat to make reform of the treaty-making system a major focus at the planned Rio de Janeiro Earth Summit of June 1992. With assistance from the Interaction Council (an informal organization of former heads of state), the Salzburg Initiative was, in fact, presented directly to a number of world leaders and distributed to several thousand activists and policymakers. The UNCED secretariat, however, was unable to push the institutional reform issue very high up the agenda at the PrepCom sessions in advance of the Rio meeting.

The Salzburg Initiative was further debated and refined at two sessions of the Salzburg Seminar, in June of 1990 and June of 1991. More than 120 governmental, nongovernmental, and corporate representatives from thirty-two countries participated in those two-week seminars chaired by an eminent team of seasoned diplomats and scholars (including the head of the Intergovernmental Panel on Climate Change, senior UNCED staff, the director-general for environment of the European Commission, senior staff from the World Wildlife Fund, the secretary-general for the Montreal Protocol negotiation, and some of the most respected international law experts in the world).

The contributors to the Salzburg Initiative agreed on several things: first, that a one-world government is neither likely nor desirable; second, that economic growth and social justice are not necessarily incompatible with sustainable development and environmental protection; third, that states are likely to retain their sovereign powers and will remain the center of global decision making; fourth, that nongovernmental interests will increasingly be called upon to play stimulative and facilitative roles that states themselves cannot perform; and, finally, that the basic structure of the United Nations will remain intact for the foreseeable future.

## The Salzburg Initiative

A great many proposals to reform the UN-sponsored system of environmental treaty making have been advanced from time to time, ranging from the creation of a worldwide environmental enforcement agency with the power to supersede national authority to more modest realignments of

UNEP, UNDP, and other multilateral agencies. The reforms outlined in the Salzburg Initiative are both different and, in many ways, more far-reaching. These proposals are convincing because they build on practice and on what we know about multiparty, multi-issue negotiation, and they do not confuse what might be desirable with what works. For example, although some experienced commentators still look at environmental treaty making as a scientifically circumscribed process aimed at solving technical problems, the authors of the Salzburg Initiative view environmental treaty making as a bargaining process focused on resolving political conflict. The issue is not what the correct technical solution is (particularly since characterization of environmental risks is based so heavily on subjective perceptions) but, rather, whether the nations of the world will work together, and if so, how.

The Salzburg Initiative contains ten recommendations:

## Recommendation 1:
## Build decentralized alliances

Clusters of countries with shared environmental interests should always be encouraged to caucus well ahead of formal treaty-making negotiations in order to explore common interests, share technical information, and analyze strategic alternatives together. Such clusters need to be assisted and encouraged by neutral conveners. For the most part, the clusters should be organized on a (bio)regional basis; that is, nations that share borders or rely on common resources should meet regularly. On other occasions, countries with common interests but without shared borders should also be encouraged to meet to exchange information and discuss the possibilities of working together to manage a resource or to respond to a threat. The point of such meetings is to build coalitions, including alliances that cut across typical North-South lines.

Coalition building of this sort should involve nongovernmental interests as well as official representatives. (N.B. This point is elaborated under Recommendation 4.) Small clusters of countries should be combined to form the core of increasingly larger coalitions that ultimately will have to bargain with other large coalitions to resolve differences.

It would be desirable to designate or create permanent (bio)regional mediation offices to serve as conveners for these coalition-building efforts. The objective of this first recommendation would be undermined, though, if identification of acceptable conveners or venues for meetings became a source of disagreement. So, to avoid the need to reinvent or debate such selections repeatedly, forums and ground rules should be set through negotiations for an extended period before any caucusing is undertaken.

Negotiations over ground rules should be managed by the UN secretary-general and the new UN Commission on Sustainable Development.

Once procedural ground rules are set, regional offices would broker the selection of individual facilitators and technical advisers for each meeting (in much the same way that federal agencies in the United States currently work from a preapproved roster of professional mediators whenever they are about to convene a regulatory negotiation).[2] Thus, the regional offices would serve a convening function, and facilitators for each session would be chosen by the parties from a preapproved roster of professional neutrals. All participating countries would have to sign off, each time, on the selection of a team of neutrals from the roster.

The United Nations (particularly UNDP) has field offices scattered throughout the world. In some regions, these offices might serve as conveners. In other instances, regional economic institutions (like the European Commission) might be selected. The choice needs to be handled differently in each part of the world. Whatever organization is selected, though, must be acceptable to the cluster of countries involved. When temporary or new clusters of noncontiguous countries are formed, the United Nations itself (that is, UNEP, UNDP, or the Commission on Sustainable Development) could serve as the convener because such clusters might only meet a few times.

This recommendation rests on the assumption that effective environmental treaty making depends on the implementation of a predictable "bottom-up" approach to aggregating increasingly larger clusters of countries and nongovernmental interests into coalitions of like-minded stakeholders. Furthermore, it presumes that treaty making does not depend primarily on convincing technical experts of the scientific merit of a particular approach to a global environmental threat. Scientific consensus building is important, but it merely informs the key exchanges among political actors who must bargain over sensitive trade-offs between short-term and long-term economic, social, and political costs and benefits. Such bargaining is particularly difficult, as is the case with global environmental treaty making, when overarching philosophical or ideological principles (like "the polluter pays") are at stake.

Building decentralized alliances on a worldwide basis is a difficult task, complicated by the desire of existing regional forums to maintain or expand their mandates. Many organizations that have been successful in bringing together groups of countries for other purposes will not be successful conveners for environmental treaty making because they have taken positions in the past that now compromise their claim to neutrality. In some regions, working relationships are in place among the countries that ought to caucus together, but nongovernmental interests still need to be blended in. And in other situations, hostile relations will no doubt make it difficult to move ahead. However, we do have the encouraging example of the Mediterranean Action Plan, which brought together (under UNEP auspices) countries that had never worked together and, indeed, between whom diplomatic relations did not exist. Because past and future relationships must be handled with great care, it matters a great deal who the conveners and facilitators are.

The costs of building new decentralized alliances should be borne by UNEP, UNDP, and the GEF, even if UN agencies are not the ones selected to play convening or facilitating roles. Although it may increase the cost, it makes sense to support as many regional and issue-oriented clusters as possible. It is perfectly acceptable for governmental and nongovernmental actors to be part of more than one convening effort. Indeed, overlap may be the key to building ever-larger coalitions, so that the smallest number of big coalitions with consistent interests can be identified. Through this process, internal differences within coalitions can be minimized, and the difficult task of generating a final agreement can be undertaken without the problems that internal conflicts within coalitions would otherwise cause.

## Recommendation 2:
## Provide prenegotiation assistance to individual countries

Only a few countries have the resources needed to develop technically and politically informed perspectives on every global issue that arises. Unfortunately, regular informational briefings are not generally available to countries that need them, nor is the strategic advice they require generally available. These could be provided by international scientific associations, transnational business organizations, leagues of nongovernmental organizations, or various branches of the United Nations. What is critical is that each country have easy access to the intelligence it needs to understand emerging problems, to assess the likely effectiveness of alternative approaches to them, and to interpret the advantages and disadvantages of alternative responses, given its political, economic, social, and ecological interests. For all the talk of capacity building, especially in the Earth Summit's Agenda 21, there is, as yet, no plan to provide this kind of support to countries that need it.

Countries with marginal legal and scientific resources need expert advice to help them prepare for both caucuses and full-fledged global negotiations. International scientific bodies (such as the Intergovernmental Panel on Climate Change, IPCC) do provide technical analysis, but they are not in a position to help individual countries interpret the strategic implications of their findings. Indeed, when the IPCC sought to summarize the implications of its research on global warming, it was accused of politicizing the issue. All efforts to make the "normative leap" from analysis to prescription are open to political challenge.

The most effective way to handle the intelligence-sharing problem would be by building on the process of regional caucusing described in the first recommendation. Joint fact-finding by mutually agreed upon advisers can help groups of countries that have shared interests but are not equipped on their own to undertake the questioning and reflection that should precede global negotiations. However, because strategic considerations preclude such openness in all situations, individual countries—even in meetings of like-minded countries and organizations—will always need confidential strategic advisers they can trust. Some national leaders are likely to oppose the presence of nongovernmental representatives at either regional caucuses or national briefing sessions. They are likely to be suspicious of all advisers who are not part of their governmental staffs. This is a shortsighted and self-defeating position (but, unfortunately, not an uncommon one). For one thing, consultants currently doing preparatory fact-finding or background research for governmental staff are often outsiders. Why, then, is it acceptable for these individuals to be involved behind the scenes, but not for other "unofficials" to attend prenegotiation briefings?

One potential solution to this problem is to require all who participate to sign a pledge of confidentiality. Persons who will not sign should not be involved. Those who violate their pledge should be excluded in the future (and so, too, should their organizations). Obviously, for countries with no tradition of democratic decision making or public access, these arguments will fall on deaf ears. However, a great many democratic nations (and those aspiring to greater openness) have not done all they can to involve nongovernmental interests during the prenegotiation phase of global environmental treaty making, either as advisers or as participants on national negotiating teams.

The presence of nongovernmental representatives can legitimize the posture a country ultimately adopts on an issue, although this is not true if the concerns of nongovernmental interests are invited but ignored. In addition, the presence of nongovernmental interests augments the spectrum of views considered when national interests are clarified and strategies are formulated. This can help even the most powerful leader anticipate national and international reactions and gauge the acceptability of various negotiating postures more effectively before public pronouncements are made. Although opening up prenegotiation sessions to nongovernmental interests can create tensions of various kinds, skilled facilitators (who may well be required to be nationals of the country in which meetings are being held) can help to manage them.

National leaders often have the same adverse reaction to involving nongovernmental interests as they do to using neutrals to facilitate pre-negotiation working sessions (fearing, above all else, that they will look weak if they relinquish control to outsiders), but savvy leaders are growing increasingly aware that "strong leadership" is not defined as an unwillingness to heed good counsel or to take advantage of the assistance of others.

## Recommendation 3:
## Adopt new approaches to treaty drafting

At present, most countries come to international conferences with their positions on all the issues completely worked out. Indeed, if they did not, they would feel and probably be viewed by their counterparts as unprepared. Moreover, because heads of state cannot always attend, envoys or delegates must be coached to represent them, which means that national positions must be clarified beforehand. Envoys are warned not to improvise; they are supposed to stick to the text prepared and approved ahead of time. Domestic leaders who have gone to great lengths to forge internal agreements before sending someone to represent them at a global conference worry about their delegates' free-lancing. What all this means, of course, is that there is not much room for improvisation. Officials and their representatives must remain faithful to the domestic promises they made, or they will lose the support of the constituencies that elected them and help keep them in power.

Thus, there is a tension between adherence to previously worked out positions and the need to be flexible and responsive when creative offers are put forward by others during negotiations. One way of reconciling that tension is to make clear that certain meetings are, in fact, only brainstorming sessions at which commitments will be neither sought nor accepted. Such gatherings should focus on the preparation of multiple drafts of potential treaties rather than just single drafts with bracketed disagreements. Possible trade-offs should be floated for discussion, but nothing should be finalized.

Much of this kind of interaction can involve "shadow" bargaining, in which a real willingness to accept certain gains or losses is masked, but skilled facilitators should be able to clarify overlapping and conflicting interests, even when the parties are not prepared to be completely candid with each other. Differences can be mapped to the point where it should be relatively easy for individual actors or groups of countries to follow up with bilateral conversations, leading to the preparation of single negotiating texts that have solid regional support and that highlight (through the use of contingent proposals) the critical disagreements that the largest coalitions will have to resolve.

It may be surprising that starting with multiple versions of a treaty can make it easier to reach consensus, but this is the case. When early multiple drafts of a treaty are prepared in a way that encourages the exploration of underlying interests as well as the formulation of creative options and trade-offs, increased opportunities for maximizing joint gains will emerge that would not otherwise materialize. The next step is for a team of neutrals to gather reactions to the multiple drafts generated at the brainstorming sessions. By "riding the circuit" and meeting privately with leaders or regional caucuses, professional neutrals should be able to synthesize a single text (and contingent proposals) to take into the final stage of negotiations. This also minimizes the need to gather large numbers of formal delegations repeatedly.

Accomplished mediators know how to build consensus among coalitions of countries that daily grow in size and diversity. At some point, though, when conflicting interests within a coalition cannot usefully be bridged, a professional neutral knows that it is time to stop. The larger coalitions that have been formed must then meet face to face, usually designating representatives for a final negotiation. This would be the most efficient and effective process of treaty drafting.

The UN system, unfortunately, has not operated in this fashion. Until recently, very small numbers of powerful nations have designated experts to prepare initial drafts. Most nations remain on the sidelines while the political giants battle it out, as they did in the Montreal Protocol negotiations. When they are finished, the others have a formal opportunity to say yes or no. The most powerful nations, however, do not speak for coalitions that have worked out internal agreements; rather, they represent their own national interests.

This dynamic changed somewhat during the series of preparation sessions that led up to the Earth Summit, and perhaps it has shifted permanently. During the PrepCom process, every country demanded a right to be present at every session, and the nongovernmental interests insisted on the right to be heard as well. The PrepComs were really committees of the whole. Very little got done, though, at most of these sessions because of the difficulty of managing 170-plus official delegations. Moreover, efforts to keep the unofficial groups on the sidelines did not work. The Earth Summit itself—with four thousand official and tens of thousands of unofficial participants—symbolizes the current negotiating situation better than anything else. This was not an efficient consensus-building model.

We seem to have moved from one extreme to the other, from a few nations or scientific organizations calling all the shots to absolutely everyone wanting a voice in all decisions. It would make more sense to move toward a decentralized, but predictable, regional system in which countries receive the support they need to prepare adequately, and the treaty-drafting process moves step by step, from multiple drafts to a single text, taking account of the need to build larger and larger coalitions.

## Recommendation 4:
## Expand the roles for nongovernmental interests

Nongovernmental interests (NGIs) have played an increasingly important part in environmental treaty making over the past twenty years. Their contributions still need to be acknowledged and formally affirmed by the United Nations. Ways of ensuring the broadest possible involvement of nongovernmental interests also need to be codified.

During the early stages of treaty negotiations, NGIs broaden the range of views expressed during the analysis of scientific, technical, and legal evidence used to diagnose the seriousness of environmental threats. They broaden the scope of the peer-review process in making sense of conflicting scientific evidence. During negotiations, sometimes without being invited, NGIs offer proposals, craft possible bargains, or work behind the scenes to "sell" a particular package. Merely by their presence, they add a degree of legitimacy to the treaties that finally emerge. In the aftermath of treaty negotiations, they can bolster the monitoring efforts of international governmental bodies by pressuring offending nations in ways that official international bodies cannot.

I do not believe that nongovernmental interests should have voting power in formal treaty making. Because few votes are ever taken in such forums, and consensus is necessary to ensure meaningful commitments on the part of signatory countries anyway, this is not a great sacrifice. In fact, voting by official delegates should be avoided, too, because it is inconsistent with the task of consensus-building.

That nongovernmental interests have the right to sit at the negotiating table is a far more significant influence on the process than granting them official voting rights. They should be active participants in treaty making for at least three reasons. First, they can—by influencing public opinion—force national leaders involved in global treaty making to take account of domestic views on an issue. Why not, therefore, bring NGIs to the table in an orderly way? When they are excluded, they are often driven to take extreme positions and to engage in harsh confrontations in order to be heard. Why not avoid this by inviting them to participate as part of national delegations at international conferences?

Second, given the importance of guaranteeing that the consensus represented by a country's signature reflects a commitment on the part of all its citizens, corporations, and organizations to change their behavior in ways consistent with new agreements, it makes sense to involve as many representatives of these groups as possible in working out the terms of a treaty. Indeed, if new accords are not responsive to the full array of concerns expressed by such groups, implementation will be thwarted or at best, difficult.

Third, nongovernmental interests can hold countries accountable for the promises they make in a treaty, but to do this successfully, they need access to monitoring data and national reports on compliance. In addition, if they are to assist in monitoring and the enforcement of a treaty, it makes sense for them to participate in setting the terms of the treaties they will be helping to enforce. This will increase their understanding of what is actually expected of them, what needs to be measured, and how monitoring results are likely to be interpreted by the other signatories.

The role of nongovernment interests in environmental treaty making should be formalized. Currently, we have a makeshift situation in which the parties to a treaty negotiate the terms of involvement for NGIs each time a new treaty-making effort is begun. We also have the continuing use of parallel "unofficial" conferences, such as the Citizens' Forum held miles apart from the formal meetings in Rio, at which counter or separate versions of each framework convention and declaration were developed. These are not productive; they undermine public confidence in the final treaties, weaken NGI support for the treaties that must be implemented, and reduce the chances that the best thinking of the NGIs will influence the final negotiations.

Full-fledged advisory and monitoring roles for nongovernmental interests would not violate the operating rules of the United Nations. Indeed, Agenda 21 calls on the secretary general of the United Nations to undertake by 1995 a complete review of the ways in which NGIs might be formally included in the environmental-treaty-making process. Although important questions remain about how specific organizations and their representatives should be selected (in response to questions about accountability), these should not be used as an excuse to keep unofficials on the sidelines any longer.

## Recommendation 5:
## Recategorize countries for the purpose of prescribing action

To avoid lowest-common-denominator responses to environmental threats, countries should be categorized by the extent to which they have caused environmental difficulties for others or by the ability and resources they have to respond. Different standards of responsibility or performance should be specified for different categories of countries in all environmental treaties.

I. William Zartman has pointed out that exceptions are currently used to get reluctant countries to accept the basic terms of new treaties. This obviously creates some unfairness because all countries in the same category are not necessarily granted the same privileges. The Montreal Protocol is often cited as the best example of categorizing countries for purposes of holding them to different standards. The protocol initially gave developing countries a ten-year "grace" period to comply with the deadline for phasing out CFCs. The grace period has been interpreted by some as a way of serving Northern industrial interests (that would have been allowed to supply the developing world with CFCs during the ten-year period), but it did differentiate among countries effectively.

We also have the precedent of groups of countries setting higher than required thresholds or earlier deadlines for the cutback of regulated substances. The group of African countries, for example, that signed the Bamaco Convention wanted to restrict the transshipment of hazardous wastes beyond the requirements of the Basel Convention because they were not satisfied with that convention. These actions are not quite the same as categorizing countries for purposes of assigning responsibility or allocating resources within the terms of a treaty. The differentiation of obligations (such as the designation of countries as members of the 30-percent-sulphur-dioxide-reduction "club" established under the 1979 Long-Range Transboundary Air Pollution Convention) is closer to the kind of categorization that is most desirable.

Each treaty-making effort ought to explore a range of country categorizations, especially when multiple treaty drafts are developed during prenegotiations. The key objective is to ensure that as many countries as possible believe that they are being treated fairly.

## Recommendation 6:
## Reinforce a better balance between science and politics

The integrity of scientific and technical analysis is undermined when it is used to justify politically expedient views. Although the interpretation of data almost always requires the application of nonobjective judgments, forecasts and models must nonetheless be credible in the eyes of those who need to take such evidence into account in making decisions. A fair sampling of scientific opinion is necessary to establish credibility. The United States, for instance, has very little impact on the thinking of other countries when it presents the views of only those scientists who remain skeptical about the problem of global warming.

All nations should help to strengthen collaborative international scientific institutions because these are more likely than national institutes to generate forecasts and analyses that will be viewed as credible by a cross-section of countries. Even here, though, there are dangers. For example, several of the IPCC working groups were sharply criticized by nongovernmental organizations when disparities in their scientific findings appeared. This may well have been caused by the fact that many IPCC delegates were government officials instructed by their ministries to ensure that certain findings did or did not emerge.

World policy-making bodies should not look to transnational scientific groups for policy recommendations or even definitive interpretations of scientific findings. These groups best serve global needs when they present the full range of scientific research, underscoring—but not attempting to resolve—the disagreements among technical experts.

Economic and ecological systems are too complex and our knowledge too primitive to permit us to predict the future with confidence. Therefore, agreements and alternative courses of action should anticipate various "futures." Treaty tightening, in this case, does not mean avoiding all prescription until irrefutable evidence is in (or a "smoking gun" is in hand); rather, it suggests that contingent strategies contained in multiple protocols should be prepared simultaneously. Stakeholders should commit to future behaviors and responsibilities that will be triggered only if certain milestones are passed. For example, the next round of climate-change protocols might require different sets of countries to cut back their emissions of certain greenhouse gases by preset amounts if, and only if, monitoring results show that quantified thresholds (measured in agreed-upon ways) have been passed. A contingency approach to handling uncertainty can yield agreements among countries and nongovernmental interests that disagree violently on how the future is likely to unfold. They do not need to agree on a forecast; they need to agree only on the responses that will be appropriate if certain events come about.

## Recommendation 7:
## Encourage issue linkage

Although there initially may be daunting institutional difficulties to overcome, the advantages of finding creative linkages across previously independent policy arenas are enormous. Linkage can generate incentives (especially economic incentives) that can change a country's calculation about whether it should come to the bargaining table or whether it should sign a particular treaty. This means that several treaties should always be negotiated simultaneously. It also means that financial arrangements indicating who will contribute to the GEF (or its successor) and who will receive assistance should always be on the table. Potential linkages between the substance of proposed environmental management treaties and various kinds of compensation may be the key to getting developing countries to accepting new regimes that they would otherwise find objectionable.

The creation of the GEF was a very important first step in this effort. The greater its scope of operations and funding, the easier it will be to use financial linkage to overcome resistance to the policy content of new treaties. Obviously, the governance of the GEF needs to be modified still further to ensure that the nations of the developing world are confident that the administrative entity in charge will be responsive to their interests. Moreover, financial compensation, while enormously helpful, is not sufficient.

The current round of negotiations over the General Agreement on Tariffs and Trade barely addressed environmental regulations, and when it did, it was only to ensure that nations did not set their environmental regulations in a way that is out of line with their trading partners. Just how this will play out, however, is not clear. Moreover, additional opportunities to make progress on environmental treaties by tying agreement to possible benefits under GATT were missed. The North American Free Trade Agreement (NAFTA) between the United States, Mexico, and Canada provides still another example of the need to link environmental protection and trade agreements. The linkage was made in the NAFTA negotiations, but the focus was primarily on "harmonizing" environmental regulations rather than on providing economic benefits in exchange for more vigorous efforts to ensure environmental quality.

If future efforts to implement climate-change protocols reach a deadlock over the imposition of a carbon tax on the use of all fossil fuels, will it be possible to make explicit adjustments in the terms of GATT to compensate countries on whom such a tax falls most heavily? Theoretically, there is nothing to prohibit this kind of linkage; indeed, trades of this sort might hold the key to breaking an impasse. The more there is to trade, the greater the chances of closing a gap between disputants.

The arguments against linkage are primarily logistical; that is, given the complexity of global negotiations it seems counterproductive to create still further complication by treating two or more separate negotiations as if they were interlocked. Orchestrating such linked negotiations implies that multiple sets of relationships can be integrated. Furthermore, once linkage is encouraged, where will it end? One of the oft-noted complaints about the General Assembly of the United Nations is that small countries regularly insist that their demands on completely unrelated matters be addressed when important international debates on other subjects are under way.

The diplomatic complexity is not likely to be as significant as it may seem at first. Moreover, the same countries will be involved in parallel negotiations whether they are officially linked or not. Indeed, because representatives from the same countries are likely to see each other repeatedly, linkages are bound to evolve. Formalizing these interconnections ought to be the task of the UN Commission on Sustainable Development. Opportunities for linkage will present themselves to the parties and succeed or not. In either case it is probably not going to be possible to write formal rules governing acceptable and unacceptable linkage. Ethical considerations (that is, demands for linkage bordering on blackmail) will be seen for what they are and brushed aside by the majority of the countries involved. Acceptable linkages are those achieved by mutual consent.

## Recommendation 8:
## Remove penalties for constructive unilateral action

Some nations fear that if they act unilaterally to tighten environmental regulations at home, they will find themselves at a competitive disadvantage when international agreements are finally signed. Indeed, some leaders have argued that their countries should wait until international accords that specify the minimum actions required are signed before they enact domestic legislation. It will be easier for them to go from having no regulation to the level required by a new treaty than it would be to ratchet up from their first level of regulation to still higher levels. The cost to a country of a first round of regulation is usually less than the cost of later efforts to reach higher levels of environmental quality.[3]

To encourage rather than discourage countries from taking positive legislative steps domestically, thresholds for gauging progress should be retroactive. That is, baselines used to assess progress should always be set several years prior to the year in which treaties are drafted so that countries that took constructive action on their own will be able to count the improvements they made toward the new treaty requirements.

In addition, regional clusters of countries should be encouraged to make informal alliances with each other, through which they can commit themselves to the proposition that actions they take after a certain date (but prior to formal global action) must be counted as progress toward any new worldwide standard. If a large enough set of countries agrees not to support any treaty that does not honor such an agreement, it can block global action. The goal, of course, is not to make it more difficult to generate agreement on new treaties but, rather, to create ongoing incentives for countries to take constructive unilateral action. Because the goal of treaty making is to push countries in this direction, such incentives would not be inappropriate.

## Recommendation 9:
## Encourage the media to play a more educative role

The mass media have a dual role to play: reporting events and educating the public. Given the increasingly important part that environmental diplomacy plays in international relations, the media must provide additional space and time for environmental news, both in anticipating coming events and in covering ongoing negotiations. The worldwide coverage of the Earth Summit was impressive, but since the end of the Rio meeting there has been little or no discussion of the serious problems that the signatories will face as they seek to implement the terms of the vague treaties that were signed.

There are several reasons that global environmental issues go unreported in many parts of the world. First, many media outlets do not have the capacity to report on such events. Few journalists have been schooled sufficiently to make these complex issues understandable. Second, the media often view their mission quite narrowly. They accept responsibility for reporting on events but not for public education. Of course, if the public is not aware of how important global environmental threats and negotiations are, they will not create a demand for such coverage. In the absence of such a demand, the media assert that the public is not interested. Ultimately, this becomes a self-fulfilling prophecy.

A worldwide network of scientific organizations and academic institutions ought to take responsibility for building an environmental data bank that the media can tap into electronically from anywhere in the world. Short midcareer training programs for potential environmental reporters ought to be available in every region. Excellence in environmental journalism, particularly for efforts to increase public awareness, ought to receive lavish praise and awards from UNEP and other international organizations.

There were thousands of credentialed members of the journalistic fraternity present at the Earth Summit, but the coverage was depressingly thin. In country after country, basic introductions to the underlying environmental risks, summaries of relevant scientific findings, and the background on the overall process of global treaty making were missing from the daily coverage of events. For the cognoscenti, there were inside reports on who said what, and who did what to whom, but for the lay public the issues were not well presented. In newspapers from ten major capitals that I reviewed during the two weeks of the Earth Summit, I was unable to find even one clearly written, informative overview of the work of the IPCC or a good explanation of the sources of scientific disagreement on the risks associated with global warming. Conversations with colleagues in a number of countries indicate that television coverage was even less impressive. We must do more to encourage the media to take its public education responsibilities seriously.

## Recommendation 10:
## No changes in the structure of the United Nations are required

The recommendations of the Salzburg Initiative can be implemented without amending the UN Charter. Although efforts to push for major realignments of the elements of the UN system may, in fact, be under way, the recommendations enumerated in the Salzburg Initiative do not require such structural change.

An independent group of current and past heads of state, including Jimmy Carter, Vaclav Havel, and Julius Nyerere has recommended that a world summit on global governance be held in 1995—the fiftieth anniversary of the founding of the United Nations—to "reexamine the organization's structure and operating procedures in light of altered world priorities and conditions since 1945." Such a reexamination might consider some of the more ambitious reforms that have been suggested by governmental and nongovernmental groups over the past few years, including a change in the composition and voting requirements of the Security Council, creation of a Red Cross–like emergency response unit (for example, a "Green Cross") with authority to intervene anywhere in response to environmental emergencies; creation of a world environmental authority to oversee and integrate international environmental and development efforts; establishment of a special environment tribunal with branches in various parts of the world; and establishment of an international environmental ombudsman, with the power to request advisory opinions from the International Court of Justice and to bring disputes before a new environmental chamber of the World Court.

Such reforms did not receive support at Rio, but there was agreement on the need to create a sustainable development commission to monitor progress on implementation of Agenda 21. The 7 June 1992 isue of the *New York Times* (p. 18) reported that this would be a "high-level watchdog group to insure that governments respect the pledges" they made at the Earth Summit and that this new international body would "rely heavily on evidence gathered by private environmental groups." The actual language of the agreement reached at the Earth Summit was somewhat more modest. Chapter 38 of Agenda 21 envisions more of a coordinating unit to pool relevant information from all parts of the United Nations. The new council would "consider information provided by governments, review progress in implementing the Agenda 21, receive and analyze relevant input from nongovernmental institutions, enhance dialogue within the UN and with outside organizations, provide appropriate recommendations to the General Assembly through the U.N.'s Economic and Social Council, and encourage capacity building."

The *Times* report implied that the new commission would operate along the lines of the UN Human Rights Commission, but this is not an explicit part of the Earth Summit agreement. Moreover, this is not the direction the new commission has chosen for itself. The report indicated that if countries do not provide the information requested, private environmental organizations like the Friends of the Earth and the World Wildlife Fund will presumably "be quick to report delinquencies, just as Amnesty International and other private human rights watchdog groups file complaints with the Human Rights Commission." It is true that the experience of the Human Rights Commission suggests that governments tend to be sensitive to public criticism, and can sometimes be made to change their policies as a result. Still, it is important to look carefully at the Human Rights Commission parallel. Will it be possible for nongovernmental organizations to monitor environmental treaty violations in the same way that Amnesty International monitors human rights abuses? Will there be clear-cut guidelines for determining whether countries are in compliance with environmental treaty requirements? Will countries that are alleged not to have met their environmental treaty obligations be shamed into compliance in the same way that countries have sometimes been when charged with human rights abuses? The answers to these questions depend less on whether the General Assembly decides to give the Commission on Sustainable Development additional powers and more on the creation of an international league of nongovernmental environmental monitoring groups modeled on Amnesty International. What is needed is a strong organizational effort to channel the energy and talent that exist now in the thousands of citizens' groups around the world into a group as influential as Amnesty International.

The General Assembly must also insist on greater coordination within the UN system. Indeed, Agenda 21 calls for an administrative committee on coordination headed by the secretary-general to provide "a vital link between the multilateral financial institutions and the other United Nations bodies at the highest administrative level." All heads of agencies must be called upon to cooperate fully with the secretary-general in order to make such a committee effective. What is most interesting about the section of Agenda 21 dealing with international institutional arrangements (Chapter 38) is that the Earth Summit participants stayed entirely within the boundaries of the existing UN structure. They devoted great care to showing how the Commission on Sustainable Development is a natural outgrowth of the Economic and Social Council's current assignments, and how the council had already been charged by the General Assembly with assisting in efforts to implement the results of the UN Conference on Environment and Development.

There is very little attention given in Agenda 21 to the steps that might be taken to give the International Court of Justice a larger role in resolving disputes surrounding the enforcement of global environmental treaties. Both the Climate Change Convention and the Biodiversity Convention assume that the World Court can and will play a dispute-resolution role, but neither convention talks about augmenting the court's capacity to do this. Establishing a special environmental chamber of the International Court of Justice might be helpful (just to handle the increased caseload resulting from the signing of new treaties), but this is not a prerequisite for effective dispute resolution. Increasing the World Court's mediating role would not require formal action of any kind. The court could make its good offices available for mediation any time it chose to do so.

Whether it is the United Nations (through UNITAR, the UN university, or some other programm) or an ad hoc consortium of universities around the world that takes the lead, it is important that an academy for environmental diplomacy be created. Such a body should serve as a training locale for national and nongovernmental representatives to build their environmental negotiation skills. It might also serve as a clearinghouse for relevant scholarly work.

## Synchronizing Worldwide Expectations

During the months preceding the Earth Summit, the negotiations over the Climate Change Convention snagged several times, usually as the result of the efforts of some countries to get others to back down or accept less. Part of the problem, though, was also the result of a serious mismatch in expectations. For some leaders, the Earth Summit was a once-in-a-lifetime opportunity to shatter the prevailing logic of Western-style economic growth, and to force the North to accept limitations on its use of world resources. For them, the negotiations over individual treaties provided an occasion to raise much larger concerns. Other leaders were more interested in consolidating support for emerging general principles—like sustainability and the "polluter pays"—so that these would become a starting point in all future environmental treaty negotiations. Still others were primarily concerned with the issue of global warming; they wanted to extract commitments that would slow the rate of global warming, or even reverse it. In sum, there were not just the usual national interests in conflict; rather, there were marked differences in expectations regarding what could and should be accomplished at the Earth Summit, or indeed in all global environmental negotiations.

In the context of the climate change and biodiversity negotiations, the Group of Seventy-seven insisted that the obligations of the developing nations should be discussed only if the developed countries agreed to provide new and additional financial resources, and to cut their emissions of greenhouse gases. The developed nations argued that they would provide new and additional financial resources only if the developing world would agree to adopt and implement national policies aimed at reducing emissions of greenhouse gases in the South, and would accept reporting provisions that allowed national claims to be monitored by outsiders. Among the industrialized countries there were differences between those favoring targets and timetables and those opposed. There was also disagreement about how much money to provide, and whether additional aid should have strings attached. Within the South, there were disagreements, too. The most significant focused on the degree to which developing countries should be required to cut emission levels and on the extent to which monitoring arrangements infringing on sovereignty should be permitted.

One hundred fifty-plus nations agreed on a formula in which the North agreed to give more money (with a bit more Southern control over its allocation) in exchange for the South's accepting a share of the responsibility for emission reductions, as well as greater accountability for the accuracy of its monitoring reports. In the end, the unwillingness of the United States to accept specific emission targets and timetables (but its willingness to add money to the Global Environmental Facility) made it easy for the South to agree to the basic trade. The Europeans, who had adopted timetables and targets for the reduction of greenhouse gas emissions before Rio, had no choice but to go along. They needed the United States and Japan to add money to the GEF, and some kind of climate convention was required to justify all the attention they had devoted to the subject, as well as the considerable costs they have taken on by adopting unilateral emission cutbacks.

I. William Zartman has suggested that all international negotiations are a matter of "the parties separately preparing and jointly identifying a formula that defines the problem in a resolvable way, and then translating the principles of the formula into specific details for implementation." The chances of arriving at a formula are limited only by each side's belief that its "minimum requirements" on priority issues must be met, and that the "maximum acceptable levels" it can offer others on the issues of greatest importance to them must not be exceeded. The search for a formula was certainly at issue in the climate-change negotiations, but the fundamental mismatch between the North and the South's expectations was not addressed. Although they found a formula, again, on a treaty-by-treaty basis, this approach may have outlived its usefulness.

Zartman suggests that the Vienna Convention on the Ozone Layer was built around a formula that offered "a loose framework agreement in exchange for research and a commitment to a workshop and future conference." In other words, proponents of stricter regulation accepted less than they wanted in exchange for a chance to get evidence that could subsequently be used to tighten the treaty. The Montreal Protocol, Zartman asserts, embodied still another formula: "variable production and consumption cutbacks in exchange for individual exceptions." Finally, the London Amendments to the Montreal Protocol offered "obligatory phaseouts in exchange for financial incentives." Zartman believes that all successful formulas offer a compromise between hard and soft camps and produce partial results that "fall forward" toward tougher binding obligations as new evidence is gathered.

From one perspective, Zartman may be right: the initial negotiations over a number of framework conventions, including the Climate Change Convention, laid out basic formulas that did not require one side to drop below its minimum or offer more than its maximum. Negotiations moved, as Zartman suggests, from "whether" to do a certain thing, in the main round, to "when, what, and how" in subsequent rounds. As this becomes a common pattern, though, some countries may find the results less and less satisfactory, especially if they are interested in moving toward a new, larger North-South bargain. If the South does not see movement toward a new global bargain, it may well refuse to accept increments in compensation in exchange for its support of additional treaties.

Expectations are now sufficiently scrambled that it is likely to become increasingly difficult to find simple formulas to overcome North-South conflicts on a treaty-by-treaty basis. At the very least, we will probably need to synchronize expectations more carefully.

## A New Three-Stage Process

I recommend that the UN General Assembly adopt a new approach to environmental treaty making that will systematize environmental treaty negotiations and synchronize global expectations.[4] More specifically, all countries should be able to rely on the fact that global environmental treaty making will move through a predictable three-stage process with explicit time limits and voting requirements. (See Table 4).

Stage I should focus primarily on scoping the threat and defining the

**Table 4   A New Three-Stage Global Environmental Treaty-Making Process**

| Stage/Purpose | Time Allotted | Vote Required | Product |
|---|---|---|---|
| I. Scoping the threat and defining the key principles that will be applied in formulating a global response. | Six months from the time that 50% of the General Assembly (GA) agrees to begin. | 50% of the General Assembly to begin; 50% of the GA must agree to go on to Stage II. | Report of scientific findings; statement of principles; signed agreement (no need to ratify). |
| II. Agreeing on general commitments, specific commitments, financial arrangements, institutional arrangements, reporting and monitoring requirements. Formulating multiple protocols with clear triggers. | Twelve months to start after Stage I is completed; twenty-four months to finish once negotiations begin; stop for twenty-four months if unsuccessful. | 50% of those who begin Stage II must ratify for it to come into force; if negotiations stop, 50% of all GA members must vote to resume. | Signed convention and multiple protocols (must be ratified). |
| III. Reviewing the results of the Stage II treaty and tightening all elements of the treaty and the protocols. | Stage III would run for three years after signing; parties would then meet again to tighten all elements and provisions of relevant protocols; continued review and further amendment always possible. | 66% of those who ratified Stage II treaty must agree to tightening amendments; delay for twenty-four months if unsuccessful; 50% of all signatories must agree to restart Stage III tightening effort. | Amended convention and amended protocols (no need to ratify). |

key *principles* (for example, the precautionary principle, the "polluter-pays" principle, the principle of sustainability, the principle of additionality in the allocation of aid) that will be applied in formulating a worldwide response to a specific problem. Each time fifty percent of the United Nations member countries agree that a risk or a threat needs to be addressed, a Stage I treaty-making process should be initiated by the UN Administrative Committee on Coordination. Stage I should be limited to six months (that is, from the time that 50 percent of the members indicate a willingness to go ahead). The goal should be a written document that summarizes the scientific basis for regarding the risk as serious and enumerates that principles that will guide the global search for an appropriate response.

Assuming Stage I is successful, Stage II should begin within one year of the time Stage I was initiated. Stage II should focus on the *general commitments* that signatories will be expected to make (such as a promise to change certain domestic policies or participate in collaborative research efforts); *specific commitments* that will apply to various categories of countries (that is, timetables, targets, and so on); *financial arrangements* that indicate who will contribute and who will receive how much money (or technology); *institutional arrangements*, including the designation of a secretariat, aimed at ensuring effective implementation; and *reporting or monitoring requirements* by which signatories will be expected to abide. All other aspects of the treaty (described in Table 2) such as the timing and mechanisms for ratification, dispute resolution techniques, and reconvening procedures should be standardized. The goal, again, should be a written document that goes beyond most framework conventions in specificity.

Negotiation for a Stage II treaty should have a twenty-four-month time limit. If fifty percent of the UN General Assembly members who begin the Stage II negotiations do not accept the result of a two-year effort, treaty making on that subject should be curtailed for at least two years. At that time, an effort could be made to start, again, if enough countries concur. The point is to cut off unproductive negotiations. Although this might appear to undercut environmental protection objectives, I think it will create tremendous pressure on the treaty advocates to work as hard as possible to meet the legitimate concerns of those who have doubts about the need for or the efficacy of a proposed new treaty. Explicit timetables and voting requirements will clarify exactly where negotiations stand at every point. The fifty percent voting required will ensure the credibility and legitimacy of the agreements that do emerge.

Assuming there is support to move forward, UN members agreeing to the Stage II treaty draft would negotiate and ratify multiple protocols, as well as describe various actions that would be taken in the future if the threat or problem disappeared or worsened. Ratification of the Stage II treaty draft plus the protocols would trigger the beginning of Stage III.

Stage III would last three years and focus on annual reviews of the reporting and monitoring results of the first several years of implementation. This would lead to recalibration of all six elements addressed in Stages I and II. A Stage III three-year learning effort would lead to treaty tightening. Stage III should run for thirty-six months after the signing of a Stage II treaty. It should occur only if two-thirds of the Stage II signatories vote to initiate a Stage III effort. If two-thirds of the countries involved at that point cannot agree, Stage III should be curtailed for at least twenty-four months, and reinstated only if at least fifty percent of all UN members agree to restart the process. Again, this will pressure those who want to move ahead to search for an acceptable formula. The product of Stage III would be a tightened treaty with a revised set of protocols to guide implementation.

Stage III treaties should contain multiple protocols (that is, contingent sets of requirements) with clear "triggers." These requirements would be revised after several years of monitoring the results of Stage III and thus would be easier to support than hypothetical requirements contained in current framework conventions. Stage III treaties would also include provisions for continued review and amendment, but these would be more likely to produce real results more of the time than the products of the existing convention-protocol system.

Such a three-stage system would have to be carefully managed, perhaps by an adequately staffed Commission on Sustainable Development, or perhaps by UNEP. It would require the full support of the UN secretary general and the General Assembly. It would allow appropriately linked treaties to be taken up simultaneously, and require capable secretariats to handle all aspects of Stage III treaty-tightening negotiations, including mediation if necessary.

A synchronized, coordinated system of this sort would allow countries and nongovernmental interests to marshal their resources so that they could participate in those aspects of specific treaty making most important to them. It would avoid the confusion and confrontation that surrounded the Climate Change, Biodiversity, and Forest negotiations during the Earth Summit. Prior to the Rio meeting, some countries (especially in Europe) were holding out for the equivalent of a Stage III climate-change treaty—including the broadest possible set of principles; requiring rigorous general and specific obligations; seeking full funding for a set of elaborate financial arrangements; creating a new institutional framework for implementation; and calling for elaborate reporting and monitoring requirements. The United States and several other countries were more interested in something closer to a Stage I treaty, with no specific obligations, no new financial requirements, and no new institutional arrangements.

Right up until the Earth Summit, the Europeans declared that they would accept nothing less than what I am calling a Stage III treaty. Indeed, a number of European leaders indicated that they would prefer to have no treaty at all rather than let the United States have the watered-down version (that is, a Stage I-type treaty with no targets or timetables) for which it was pushing. The United States insisted on the equivalent of a Stage I treaty or nothing, and without the financial commitment of the United States, a basic bargain was out of reach.

The three-stage approach I am recommending would avoid this kind of confrontation, and permit step-by-step movement on a predictable schedule toward the best possible treaty or package of treaties. As it stands now, we have no idea when or whether there will be follow-up protocols to the Climate Change Convention. Although the agreements signed in Rio call for a follow-up conference of the signatories by 1999 (to review national reports on what countries are doing to reduce the emission of greenhouse gases), there is no guarantee that fifty nations will actually ratify the treaty or that when they do meet, there will be scientific evidence that allows them to "fall forward" to a binding set of emission targets and timetables. For all we know, the Earth Summit might mark the last worldwide effort to push for sustainable development. A more predictable schedule and voting system would guard against this possibility.

The most important differences between the traditional convention-protocol approach as it has evolved over the past decade and the three-stage process I am proposing have to do with predictability. The three-stage process would operate on a schedule that everyone would know ahead of time. The votes required to move through the process would be clear (and decisions would not require unanimity). The elements included in each treaty would not vary, nor would the criteria for measuring adequate progress (or for halting the treaty-making process). Greater predictability would allow the United Nations, all of its members, and non-governmental groups interested in participating in treaty making to target their resources, organize their preparatory and coalition-building efforts, and anticipate potential linkages among treaty-making efforts scheduled during the same window in time.

Let me anticipate several challenges to my three-stage process. First, some participants will argue that the schedule I propose is artificial, and that the current open-ended process provides helpful flexibility. They prefer to let each treaty-making effort run its course. My view is that we pay too high a price for such flexibility. Prior to the Earth Summit, the complaint was that treaty making took too long—often a decade or more from the point at which scientific meetings started until the first round of treaty tightening produced a meaningful protocol. Preparations for the Earth Summit went too fast, allowing to little time for consensus building on a range of meaningful commitments (for example, timetables, targets, and financial arrangements). The schedule I describe, or something like it, offers a reasonable middle ground.

Some nongovernmental organizations will suggest that the voting thresholds I am suggesting may bring a halt to all environmental treaty making. They are willing to continue the current practice of having only small groups of countries work on and sign certain conventions so that there is at least some action in the face of significant threats. I am more concerned than they are about the implementability and effectiveness of treaties that do not represent genuine commitments by large segments of the world's population.

Finally, there are likely to be critics of the three-stage process who will argue that what I am proposing is not that different from the current treaty-making system. It still presupposes national sovereignty and a continuation of the one-country, one-vote system in the United Nations. It offers no guarantee of collective action in the face of serious threats. It still presumes five to eight years will be required to build support for the equivalent of tightened protocols. These criticisms are correct, but they underestimate the significance of the key differences.

The synchronization of worldwide expectations and adoption of the three-stage approach would accomplish three important goals. First, the all-or-nothing quality of the Rio debates would be avoided. Because the steps in the process would be clear (and the later phases and voting rules inevitable), countries would not have to be so demanding in the early stages of treaty negotiations. The Climate Change Convention was almost scuttled because too many battles were being fought by countries that thought they had to win all their key points in this one negotiation (for fear there might not be subsequent negotiations on global warming). Second, the three-stage approach facilitates issue linkage and encourages adoption of contingent protocols. Without a clear picture and overall management of the broader treaty-making agenda, effective linkage and contingent protocols are much harder to achieve. Finally, the three-stage process creates an explicit collaborative learning process. The primary function of monitoring is for treaty adjustment and improvement rather than ensuring compliance. This creates a more constructive environment and ought to improve working relationships.

The three-stage process addresses the North-South split by making an overarching global bargaining effort possible. A more predictable and organized treaty-making system will make this metalevel of negotiation more explicit. The three-stage approach addresses the sovereignty issue by making it easier for nongovernmental organizations to participate effectively in treaty making. Moreover, many smaller countries should be less defensive because the voting thresholds guarantee that a few large countries will not be able to bully them or go ahead without them. The three-stage process increases the incentives to bargain, in part, because the risk of being co-opted is less when the steps and voting thresholds are explicit. In part, participating in Stage I negotiations requires no prior commitment to join Stage II. More countries will have a chance to learn about possible environmental threats and address larger questions of principle without having to make any commitments or implied commitments to take action.

A move to the three-stage process will do two other things. It will strengthen the hand of secretariats by giving them a clear mandate and making it clear that consensus-building is the goal. It will also make it easier for the UN secretary-general to maintain a five-year management perspective on negotiations concerning global environmental treaties. Now, because of the haphazard nature of the treaty-making process, scheduling and budgeting are next to impossible.

## What We Need from the United Nations

Over the next few years, as the fiftieth anniversary of the United Nations approaches, there is likely to be a great deal of attention focused on the need to reform the array of multilateral institutions that has emerged willy-nilly. The Stockholm Initiative, by Jimmy Carter and other world leaders, calling for a world summit on global governance, may help to crystallize the reform agenda. My guess is, though, that environmental issues will not drive these discussions; instead, the operations of world economic institutions and the need to redefine the peacemaking and peacekeeping roles of the United Nations are more likely to receive the greatest attention.

If these debates bog down, as I believe they will, in a battle between those who favor a tilt toward world governance and those who are as committed as ever to national sovereignty, it should not affect the chances of moving forward with the reforms contained in the Salzburg Initiative or the adoption of new UN bylaws embodying the three-stage process for global environmental treatymaking. Nor should such a debate affect the work of the Commission of Sustainable Development, the strengthening of UNEP, or a push for greater coordination among UN agencies involved in sustainable development efforts.

The Commission on Sustainable Development is a natural outgrowth of the Brundtland Commission's efforts and is legitimized by the accords signed at the Earth Summit. The Rio Declaration fell far short of the Earth Charter originally envisioned by the UNCED secretary-general, but the General Assembly may still decide to use it as the basis for an environmental declaration on a par with the Universal Declaration of Human Rights, And, even if it does not rewrite international law (the way the Brundtland Commission recommended), it may still be a very important piece of the new machinery that the Commission on Sustainable Development creates to implement Agenda 21.

The creation of the new commission in no way minimizes the need to expand the operations of UNEP, which must have additional resources and an expanded mandate so it can operate as more of an executive agency. There is an enormous amount of substantive (as opposed to administrative) work that needs to be done on global environmental management, and UNEP is the agency with the experience to do it. I am thinking particularly of the basic ecological research that must be encouraged and coordinated so that future environmental treaty making rests on a more solid scientific foundation.

Greater coordination among UN agencies involved in sustainable development activities also can move ahead through informal interagency agreements that require no change in the UN Charter. The changing role of the World Bank and UNDP, represented by their collaboration in the GEF, needs to be codified. The long-term financing of the GEF, unresolved at the Earth Summit, must be revisited. Whether it is the 0.7 percent of GNP target or some other method of collecting ODA, the GEF must be put on a permanent and automatic financial footing. The UN agencies should probably create jointly run technical assistance centers in each region of the world. UNEP, UNDP, GEF, the World Bank, and other agencies could operate out of these shared field offices. This can be done in conjunction with nongovernmental organizations or regional economic institutions as appropriate.

The General Assembly will need to clarify the role it envisions for nongovernmental organizations in global environmental treaty making. As Marc Levy, Robert Keohane, and Peter Haas have written in their extensive study of international environmental institutions, nongovernmental organizations have key roles to play in "increasing nongovernmental concern, enhancing the contractual environment, and increasing national capacity."[5] NGOs can be called upon to disseminate scientific knowledge, increase public awareness of environmental threats, provide bargaining forums, help with monitoring, increase national and international accountability, and help to transfer management and technical expertise. To accomplish these tasks, they must maintain their independence, although this does not mean that they cannot play a role on national delegations or sit at the table in international negotiations.

One of the most radical reforms of the United Nations I have heard of thus far would involve the creation of a bicameral decision-making system for world governance—a lower house of regional representatives elected or selected by constituencies of all kinds and an upper house of national representatives. Just how these two houses would operate in relation to each other is not clear, nor has anyone suggested a mechanism for choosing a manageable number of delegates to the lower house. Yet, the intention is clear. What is surprising, I think, is that the advantages of such a bicameral system for global decision making over the reforms I have suggested are not immediately apparent. There is a great deal that can be done to increase the effectiveness and responsiveness of the UN system that does not require radical reform.

Most of the important environmental management issues over the next century are likely to be global rather than regional or local. To address these effectively, new ways of enabling international cooperation will be required. To the extent that national sovereignty remains in place, the reforms outlined above offer both a rationale and the means needed to ensure more effective global environmental treaty making.

# Selected Global Environmental Treaties

| Name of Treaty | Environmental Threat Targeted | Proposed Response | Major Points of Contention | Year Treaty Signed | Number of Signatories at Time of Signing |
|---|---|---|---|---|---|
| 1 *International Convention for the Regulation of Whaling* | Depletion of stocks of commercially harvested whale species (N.B., convention was not established for conservation purposes). | Parties required to implement regulations and decisions arising from annual meeting of IWC on infractions. Complete catch reports required from members engaged in subsistence and scientific whaling. Whale harvest declines from 38,977 in 1970 to 688 in 1990. | Originally, size of kill quotas. In 1970s and early 1980s, whether to ban whaling. Ban on "scientific" whaling sought by conservation groups and anti-whaling convention parties. Presently, Iceland, Norway, and Japan seeking IWC sanction to resume commercial whaling. | Dec. 2, 1946 | 9 |
| 2 *Antarctic Treaty* | Environmental damage resulting from military activities, nuclear waste, and radioactive waste dumping. | Voluntary compliance. Undertake scientific research without damaging Antarctic environment, and in a spirit of cooperative endeavor between contracting parties. | Sovereignty claims (frozen by Treaty) and requirements for consultative status (versus observer status). Developing nations contend Antarctic Treaty system membership conditions are exclusionary. | Dec. 1, 1959 | 12 |
| Agreed Measures on the Conservation of Ant- | Exploitation of fauna and flora, infection of Ant- | Voluntary regulation with use of permit system to | Limited harvesting sought by some nations. Pollu- | June 13, 1964 | 12 |

(continued)

**Appendix A** (*Continued*)

| Name of Treaty | Number of Signatories Today | Date Treaty Came into Force | Secretariat | Major Treaty Adjustments | Monitoring Arrangements |
|---|---|---|---|---|---|
| 1 *International Convention for the Regulation of Whaling* | 37 | Nov 10, 1948 | International Whaling Commission. Responsibilities: determine, on the basis of scientific findings, whether whaling shoud occur and if so, by whom, which species, where, when, and at what levels (quota system applicable). | Numerous amendments over life of convention. Most notable was 1982 decision approving phaseout of commercial whaling over three-year period. Ban became effective in 1986 and remains in place today. | Self regulation—Convention signatories required to report on all issues relevant to implementation of Convention requirements. Compliance monitored by national inspectors and international observers and enforced de facto by risk of damaging goodwill and trade. |
| 2 *Antarctic Treaty* | 40 | Jun 23, 1961 | None: consensus procedures employed at annual consultative meetings. | Development of additional specific sub-treaties/ protocols in 1964, 1972, 1980, 1988. | Surprise inspections can be carried out by any Treaty member. Advance notice of all expeditions is mandatory. |
| Agreed Measures on the Conservation of Ant- | 12 | July 27, 1966 | Antarctic Treaty Parties | Superseded by CCAMLR in 1980 and more re- | Voluntary regulation, each contracting party re- |

(*continued*)

| Name of Treaty | Environmental Threat Targeted | Proposed Response | Major Points of Contention | Year Treaty Signed | Number of Signatories at Time of Signing |
|---|---|---|---|---|---|
| ...arctic Fauna and Flora of the Continent | arctic fauna with disease from imported domestic fauna (sled dogs and poultry). | "take" flora and/or fauna. | tion by scientific research and tourism. | | |
| Convention for the Conservation of Antarctic Seals | Commercial exploitation of Antarctic seals. | Voluntary compliance. No taking of specified seal species except in accordance with Convention Provisions. Parties obligated to adopt regulations necessary for implementing the Convention. | Some nations seeking reestablishment of commercial sealing. | June 1, 1972 | 12 |
| Convention for the Conservation of Antarctic Marine Living Resources (CCAMLR) | Degradation of marine ecosystem surrounding Antarctic continent and overexploitation of marine resources. | Compliance with regulatory measures, including quotas on all commercial species (legally binding). | Krill harvesting—quotas and access to resource. Pollution by scientific research and pollution. | May 20, 1980 | 15 |

(*continued*)

**Appendix A** (*Continued*)

| Name of Treaty | Number of Signatories Today | Date Treaty Came into Force | Secretariat | Major Treaty Adjustments | Monitoring Arrangements |
|---|---|---|---|---|---|
| arctic Fauna and Flora of the Continent | | (part) Sept 1, 1966 (whole) | | cently by the 1991 protocol on environmental protection. | quired to inform others of all activities relevant to implementation of Agreed Measures. |
| Convention for the Conservation of Antarctic Seals | 15 | Mar 11, 1978 | Antarctic Treaty Parties. | Amendment agreed to Sept. 12–16, 1988. | Contracting Parties required to inform each other when permits to take seals are issued and to meet every five years to review the Convention's operations. |
| Convention for the Conservation of Antarctic Marine Living Resources (CCAMLR) | 27 | Apr 7, 1982 | CCAMLR—facilitates research; data gathering analysis and dissemination; compliance with Convention requirements; formulation, adoption, and revision of conservation measures and implementa- | New conservation measures adopted in 1990. | Each party required to report any activities in violation of Convention, Observation and inspection system in place to verify compliance with measures adopted in 1990. |

(*continued*)

| Name of Treaty | Environmental Threat Targeted | Proposed Response | Major Points of Contention | Year Treaty Signed | Number of Signatories at Time of Signing |
|---|---|---|---|---|---|
| Convention on the Regulation of Antarctic Mineral Resources Activities (CRAMRA) | Degradation of Antarctic ecosystem by mining. | Control over extent and nature of mineral exploration/exploitation. | Disagreement over whether to ban mineral exploration/exploitation completely. | June 2, 1988 | 20 |
| Protocol on Environmental Protection | Degradation of Antarctic environment by mineral exploration/exploitation. | By complying with legally binding 50 year moratorium on mineral exploration and exploitation, ATS Parties will be required to achieve "Comprehensive protection of the Antarctic environment and its dependent and associated ecosystems." | Opposition from U.S. resulted in 50-year moratorium instead of permanent protection proposed by other parties. | 1991 | 40 |

(continued)

Appendix A  (Continued)

| Name of Treaty | Number of Signatories Today | Date Treaty Came into Force | Secretariat | Major Treaty Adjustments | Monitoring Arrangements |
|---|---|---|---|---|---|
| | | | tion of observation and inspection system. | | |
| Convention on the Regulation of Antarctic Mineral Resources Activities (CRAMRA) | 26 | 1991 | Collective management by 38 Member States of ATCP. | Moved from a position supporting controlled mineral exploration/exploitation in 1988 to a 50-year moratorium effective from 1991 (Protocol on Environmental Protection). | Self enforcement by ATCP. |
| Protocol on Environmental Protection | 40 | Not yet in force | None: consensus procedures employed at annual consultative meetings. | Puts into place many recommendations from other Conventions of the Antarctic Treaty System in addition to establishing new rules and institutions. Also foreshadows establishment of advisory Environmental Committee. | Surprise inspections can be carried out by any treaty member. Advance notice of all expeditions is mandatory. All parties required to report annually on steps taken to implement Protocol. |

(continued)

| Name of Treaty | Environmental Threat Targeted | Proposed Response | Major Points of Contention | Year Treaty Signed | Number of Signatories at Time of Signing |
|---|---|---|---|---|---|
| 3 *Treaty Banning Nuclear Weapons Tests in the At-mosphere, in Outer Space, and Underwater* | Radioactive contamination beyond jurisdictional boundary of nation conducting test, particularly through atmospheric dispersion. | Banning of above ground testing of nuclear weapons. Radiation threat from atmospheric contamination has declined substantially since 1963 ban. | Does not cover underground testing. Of signatories to the Treaty, only the USA, France, and the former USSR oppose a complete ban on all forms of testing. | Aug. 5, 1963 | 117 |
| 4 *Convention on Wetlands of International Importance Especially as Waterfowl Habitat (RAMSAR)* | Wetlands degradation and loss. | Designation of one national wetland for inclusion in a "List of Wetlands of International Importance" and plan for protection of listed wetland. Establish wetland reserves and cooperate in management of shared wetlands and wetland species. | Lack of commitment by developed countries to provide financial and technical assistance to developing countries. Level of funding promised has not been forthcoming. | Feb 2, 1971 | 7 |

(*continued*)

| Name of Treaty | Number of Signatories Today | Date Treaty Came into Force | Secretariat | Major Treaty Adjustments | Monitoring Arrangements |
|---|---|---|---|---|---|
| 3 Treaty Banning Nuclear Weapons Tests in the Atmosphere, in Outer Space, and Underwater | 118 | Oct. 10, 1963 | None. | None. | Prior to breakup of USSR, annual on-site inspections were undertaken to verify compliance. |
| 4 Convention on Wetlands of International Importance Especially as Waterfowl Habitat (RAMSAR) | 65 | Dec 21, 1975 | Ramsar Convention Bureau (IUCN): meets regularly with secretariats of other international conventions on nature conservation. | Amendments on Dec. 3, 1982—effective Oct. 1, 1985. Further amendment agreed in 1987. | Parties required to report to each Conference of Contracting Parties, also if ecological character of a listed site is changing or expected to change. Monitoring procedure instigated in 1988. |

(*continued*)

**Appendix A** (*Continued*)

| Name of Treaty | Environmental Threat Targeted | Proposed Response | Major Points of Contention | Year Treaty Signed | Number of Signatories at Time of Signing |
|---|---|---|---|---|---|
| 5 *Convention on the Prevention of Marine Pollution by Dumping of Wastes and Other Matter* (*London Dumping Convention*) | Ocean dumping of high-level radioactive wastes and other pollutants. | Prevention of oceanic pollution caused by dumping. Application of measures required to implement Convention through enforcement of prohibition on dumping of specified (high toxicity) pollutants. Permit system required for some (lower level toxicity) pollutants. | Permissible dumping levels. Extent of compliance by Parties with Convention requirements. Monitoring and enforcement logistics. Time frames for implementation of moratoriums. | Dec 29, 1972 | 31 |
| 6 *Convention Concerning the Protection of the* | Destruction of internationally significant sites | Provision of emergency and long-term pro- | Primarily within each state in terms of what should | Nov 23, 1972 | 20 |

(*continued*)

**Appendix A** (*Continued*)

| Name of Treaty | Number of Signatories Today | Date Treaty Came into Force | Secretariat | Major Treaty Adjustments | Monitoring Arrangements |
|---|---|---|---|---|---|
| 5 *Convention on the Prevention of Marine Pollution by Dumping of Wastes and Other Matter (London Dumping Convention)* | 66 | Sep 30, 1975 | International Maritime Organization (IMO) responsibilities—convene consultative meetings; facilitate communications between Parties; determine exceptional and emergency procedures. | 1983—Ban placed on further dumping of low-level radioactive wastes until proven safe (extended in 1985 and 1988—until 1992); 1990—agreement to halt all industrial waste dumping by 1995 (including subseabed nuclear waste disposal). | Parties can enforce Convention in Territorial waters. Parties required to inform IMO of all Convention controlled dumping and oceanic monitoring undertaken. Compliance monitored at consultative meetings (no non-compliance procedures in place). |
| 6 *Convention Concerning the Protection of the* | 123 | Dec 17, 1975 | UNESCO—World Heritage Bureau, works | None. | No inspection or specific reporting process estab- |

(*continued*)

**Appendix A**  (*Continued*)

| Name of Treaty | Environmental Threat Targeted | Proposed Response | Major Points of Contention | Year Treaty Signed | Number of Signatories at Time of Signing |
|---|---|---|---|---|---|
| *World Cultural and National Heritage* | having outstanding natural and/or cultural value. | tection for cultural and natural features of outstanding universal values. | be nominated. | | |
| 7 *Convention on International Trade in Endangered Species (CITES)* | Overexploitation/extinction of endangered species of flora and fauna through international trade. | Ban trade in Appendix I listed species. Control trade in Appendix II species by import/export permit system. Establish Management and Scientific Authorities. Elephant poaching declined by 80 percent in months after 1990 ban on ivory trading. | Categories in which species are included, particularly those with commercial values. Countries with well-managed elephant populations are lobbying for lifting of ban. | Mar 3, 1973 | 96 |

(*continued*)

**Appendix A** (*Continued*)

| Name of Treaty | Number of Signatories Today | Date Treaty Came into Force | Secretariat | Major Treaty Adjustments | Monitoring Arrangements |
|---|---|---|---|---|---|
| *World Cultural and National Heritage* | | | closely with IUCN and International Waterfowl and Wetlands Research Bureau (IWRB). | | lished. IUCN and UNESCO measure compliance of State Parties to specific commitments given under procedures for monitoring of the condition and conservation status of World Heritage properties. |
| 7 *Convention on International Trade in Endangered Species (CITES)* | 114 | Jul 1, 1975 | UNEP/CITES or World Conservation Union—formerly the IUCN (International Union for the Conservation of Nature). | Amendment protocols; Bonn 1979 (financial provisions); Gaborone, 1983 (relating to accession to Convention by regional economic integration organizations); African elephant upgraded from Appendix II to I in 1989—ban instigated on trade in ivory products. | Convention members required to forward annual report and trade records to secretariat, as well as biennial report on legislative, regulatory, and administrative measures taken. |

(*continued*)

| Name of Treaty | Environmental Threat Targeted | Proposed Response | Major Points of Contention | Year Treaty Signed | Number of Signatories at Time of Signing |
|---|---|---|---|---|---|
| 8 International Convention for the Prevention of Pollution from Ships (MARPOL) | Oceanic and coastal zone pollution resulting from ships discharging waste (over 400 specified pollutants) at sea. | Parties required to prevent pollution by implementing provisions of Convention, specifically; to prohibit violations and prosecute violators; to apply the provisions so as not to ensure more favorable treatment of non-parties; and to cooperate in enforcement. | Opposed by shipping interests 1973 MARPOL not implemented because of dispute over provisions for hazardous chemicals transports. | Mov. 2, 1973 | 53 |
| 9 Convention on the Conservation of Migratory Species of Wild Animals (CMS) | Transboundary degradation of migratory species habitat and population stock. | Adherence to agreements of Convention with respect to prohibiting taking of Appendix I endangered species. Endeavor to conserve habitats of these species and to conclude agreements benefitting Appendix II species. | Fails to make special provision for developing nations except for nonbinding resolution to assist with financial aid. Amount of funding promised has not been forthcoming. | June 23, 1979 | 15 |

(continued)

164

**Appendix A** (*Continued*)

| Name of Treaty | Number of Signatories Today | Date Treaty Came into Force | Secretariat | Major Treaty Adjustments | Monitoring Arrangements |
| --- | --- | --- | --- | --- | --- |
| 8 *International Convention for the Prevention of Pollution from Ships (MARPOL)* | 68 | Oct 2, 1983 | MARPOL c/o International Maritime Organization (IMO): receives reports, general administration, and consideration of amendments to the Convention and its Annexes. | Evolved from International Convention for the Prevention of Pollution of the Sea by Oil (1954). Modified in 1978 by separating requirements for different pollutants. | MARPOL members required to report all infractions, enforcement, and statistics on effectiveness of regulations. No data is collected on compliance with either operational or technical regulations. |
| 9 *Convention on the Conservation of Migratory Species of Wild animals (CMS)* | 39 | Nov 1, 1983 | UNEP/CMS Administrative and financial responsibilities. Dispute settlement mechanism available. | Development of agreements for particular species. | Parties required to report measures taken to implement Convention agreements. No observation or inspection process in place. |

(*continued*)

**Appendix A** *(Continued)*

| Name of Treaty | Environmental Threat Targeted | Proposed Response | Major Points of Contention | Year Treaty Signed | Number of Signatories at Time of Signing |
|---|---|---|---|---|---|
| 10 *"Convention on Long Range Transboundary Air Pollution"* | Acid rain. | Geneva—no effective regulatory requirements. | Source of problem. Magnitude of problem. Extent of remedial action required. | Nov. 13, 1979—Geneva | 34 |
| *"Protocol on the Reduction of Sulfur Emissions or their Transboundary Fluxes by at least 30%"* | | Helsinki—requirements to reduce 1980 $SO_2$ levels by 1993. | Responsibilities for remediation. Time frame for action. | July 9, 1985—Helsinki | 20 |
| *"Protocol Concerning the Control of Emissions of Nitrogen Oxides or their Transboundary Fluxes"* | | Sofia—requirements to freeze $NO_2$ levels or transboundary flows to 1987 levels with concessions for most countries to postpone compliance until 1994. | | Nov. 1, 1988—Sofia | 29 |
| *"Protocol Concerning the Control of Emissions of Volatile Organic Compounds or their Transboundary Fluxes"* | | Geneva—implement additional controls over emissions of volatile organic compounds. | | Nov. 18, 1991—Geneva | 21 |

*(continued)*

| Name of Treaty | Number of Signatories Today | Date Treaty Came into Force | Secretariat | Major Treaty Adjustments | Monitoring Arrangements |
|---|---|---|---|---|---|
| 10 *"Convention on Long Range Transboundary Air Pollution"* | Geneva '79—34 (33 ratified) | Geneva '70—Mar. 16, 1983 | Geneva—Secretariat under the ECE (United Nations Economic Commission for Europe). | Evolved from Geneva Convention in 1979 to Helsinki Protocol in 1985 to Sofia Protocol in 1988 and Geneva Protocol in 1991. A Protocol on Long Term Financing of the Cooperative Programme for Monitoring and Evaluation of the Long-Range Transmission of Air Pollutants in Europe (EMEP) was concluded in 1984 (31 ratifying parties). | Convention signatories required to report all issues related to domestic implementation. Technical monitoring undertaken independently by EMEP (Cooperative Program for Monitoring and Evaluation of the Long-Range Transmission of Air Pollutants in Europe). |
| *"Protocol on the Reduction of Sulfur Emissions or their Transboundary Fluxes by at least 30%"* | Helsinki—20 | Helsinki—Sept. 2, 1987 | | | |
| *"Protocol Concerning the Control of Emissions of Nitrogen Oxides or their Transboundary Fluxes"* | Sofia—29 signatories (18 ratifiers) | Sofia—Feb. 14, 1991 | | | |
| *"Protocol Concerning the Control of Emissions of Volatile Organic Compounds or their Transboundary Fluxes"* | Geneva '91—23 | Geneva '91—not yet in force | | | |

(continued)

**Appendix A**  (*Continued*)

| Name of Treaty | Environmental Threat Targeted | Proposed Response | Major Points of Contention | Year Treaty Signed | Number of Signatories at Time of Signing |
|---|---|---|---|---|---|
| 11 *United Nations Convention on the Law of the Sea (UNCLOS)* | • Marine pollution<br>• Unsustainable management of marine resources | Each Party must: monitor potentially damaging activities they engage in and report results to relevant International Organizations, enforce national and international standards regarding pollution created under their jurisdiction. Treaty also seeks to provide for equitable sharing of seabed mineral resources outside national marine boundaries. | Disagreement on deep seabed mining provisions, notably production policy, compensation fund, financial terms of contracts, and environmental considerations. | Dec 10, 1982 | 157 original signatories, but only 51 ratifying parties. |
| 12 *Vienna Convention for the Protection of the Ozone Layer* | Depletion of Ozone layer. | No obligations to act: agreement to cooperate on monitoring, research, and data exchange only. Global CFC consumption declined from 1.2 | Disagreement on extent of problem. Decreased production opposed by major producing states (veto coalition). | Mar 22, 1985 | 28 |

(continued)

| Name of Treaty | Number of Signatories Today | Date Treaty Came into Force | Secretariat | Major Treaty Adjustments | Monitoring Arrangements |
|---|---|---|---|---|---|
| 11 *United Nations Convention on the Law of the Sea (UNCLOS)* | 157 signatories 51 ratifications as of Dec. 1991 | Not yet in force—will enter into force 12 months after ratification by 60 countries | Division for Ocean Affairs and Law of the Sea—UN Office of Legal Affairs. | Though not yet in force, the Convention's principal objectives have been incorporated into most related global and regional Treaties. National laws of many Parties and mandates of related organizations have been amended in conformity with the Convention. | Parties report within United Nations annual report on the Law of the Sea and UN General Assembly. Formal protest notes against contraventions by other states published in Law of the Sea Bulletin. No observation/inspection process presently operational. |
| 12 *Vienna Convention for the Protection of the Ozone Layer* | 98 | Sep 22, 1988 | UNEP Ozone Secretariat. | Strengthened by adoption of Montreal Protocol. | Parties report to Secretariat on measures undertaken in scientific research and cooperation. |

*(continued)*

**Appendix A** *(Continued)*

| Name of Treaty | Environmental Threat Targeted | Proposed Response | Major Points of Contention | Year Treaty Signed | Number of Signatories at Time of Signing |
|---|---|---|---|---|---|
| Montreal Protocol on Substances That Deplete the Ozone Layer | Depletion of Ozone layer. | billion/kg peak in 1987 to estimated .682 billion/kg in 1991. As amended in 1990—total phaseout of specified list of CFCs, halons, carbon tetrachlorides by 2000; methyl chloroform by 1995. Scheduled interim reductions for each chemical (CFCs–50% by '95, 85% by '97, 100% by 2000) Assess control measures every 4 years. | Disagreement on extent of problem, level of production cuts required, and provision of aid to developing nations to enable compliance with phaseout targets. | Sep 16, 1987 | 46 (15 ratified original agreement) |
| 13 *Convention on the Control of Transboundary Movements of Hazardous* | Quantity of hazardous waste produced; methods of disposal; quan- | Exporting countries must provide importing country with detailed data on | Opposition from major recipient countries, particularly African States. | Mar 22, 1989 | 53 |

*(continued)*

| Name of Treaty | Number of Signatories Today | Date Treaty Came into Force | Secretariat | Major Treaty Adjustments | Monitoring Arrangements |
|---|---|---|---|---|---|
| Montreal Protocol on Substances That Deplete the Ozone Layer | 75—1987 agreement 93—1990 amendment | Jan 1, 1989 1990—amendment is not yet in force | UNEP Ozone Secretariat (United Nations Environment Program) Secretariat of Interim Multilateral Ozone Fund (administers Trust Fund). | 1989—80 nations vote for total CFC phaseout by 2000 (nonbinding declaration). Amendment signed Jun '90—installs 1997 phaseout deadline. Phaseout times for additional ozone depleting chemicals and financial mechanism for implementation also established. | Reporting requirements on production and trade (with Parties and non-Parties) in controlled substances. |
| 13 *Convention on the Control of Transboundary Movements of Hazardous* | 56 (17 ratifications by | May 5, 1992 | UNEP/Interim Secretariat for the Basel Convention. | 1989 (Lome IV Convention)—12 EC countries sign ten year pact ban- | Each Party to report to Conference of Parties on steps taken to imple- |

(*continued*)

**Appendix A**  (*Continued*)

| Name of Treaty | Environmental Threat Targeted | Proposed Response | Major Points of Contention | Year Treaty Signed | Number of Signatories at Time of Signing |
|---|---|---|---|---|---|
| *Wastes and Their Disposal (Basel Convention)* | tities moved across international boundaries and procedures for movement; and safety requirements and procedures for storage of hazardous wastes in importing countries. | waste shipment and importing country must have provided prior written consent. | Also concern expressed by Environmental groups about weakness of Convention regulations. | | |
| 14 *Biodiversity Convention* | Species extinction on the global scale. | Development of plans to protect habitat and species, provide funds and technological assistance to help developing countries provide protection, ensure commercial access to biological resources and share derived benefits, establish biotechnology safety regulations. | Nature of commitments entreated in financial assistance mechanism, mechanism for sharing benefits, nature of biotechnology regulations. | June 1992 (Rio de Janeiro) | 153 |

(*continued*)

| Name of Treaty | Number of Signatories Today | Date Treaty Came into Force | Secretariat | Major Treaty Adjustments | Monitoring Arrangements |
|---|---|---|---|---|---|
| *Wastes and Their Disposal (Basel Convention)* | the end of 1991) | | | ning waste shipment to 69 African, Caribbean, and Pacific countries who also agree to ban any waste imports. 1991 (Bamako Convention)—12 (now 18) African states ban the import of hazardous wastes. | ment Convention requirements. Conference of Parties is required to continuously review and evaluate effectiveness of Convention implementation. |
| 14 *Biodiversity Convention* | 153 | Not yet in force | Secretariat under the umbrella of the UNCED. Financial assistance mechanism to be administered by the Global Environment Facility in the interim. | None since signing. | None yet established. |

(*continued*)

**Appendix A**  *(Continued)*

| Name of Treaty | Environmental Threat Targeted | Proposed Response | Major Points of Contention | Year Treaty Signed | Number of Signatories at Time of Signing |
|---|---|---|---|---|---|
| 15 *The Convention on Climate Change* | Global Climate Change. | Developed Countries: return to "earlier" emission levels by 2000, development of national emission limits and inventories, report on progress. Developing nations: report on status quo and if possible on mitigation measures taken. | Extent of problem, specific reduction requirements, time frame for implementation, onus for action. | June 1992 (Rio de Janeiro) | 153 |

*(continued)*

**Appendix A** *(Continued)*

| Name of Treaty | Number of Signatories Today | Date Treaty Came into Force | Secretariat | Major Treaty Adjustments | Monitoring Arrangements |
|---|---|---|---|---|---|
| 15 *The Convention on Climate Change* | 153 | Not yet in force | Secretariat under the umbrella of the UNCED. Financial assistance mechanism to be administered by the Global Environment Facility in the interim. | Specific commitments to limit emissions of carbon dioxide diluted to more general non-specific wording immediately prior to Rio Conference. | Compliance requirements relatively loose for developing countries. |

*Sources:*

Gareth Porter and Janet Brown, *Global Environmental Politics* (Boulder, Colorado: Western Press, 1991).

Helga Ole Bergesen, Magnor Norderharg, and George Parmann, (eds.), *Green Globe Yearbook 1992* (Oxford: Oxford University Press, 1992).

Caroline F. Thomas, *The Environment in International Relations* (London: Royal Institute of International Affairs, 1992).

Hillary French, "*After the Earth Summit: The Future of Environmental Governance,*" *Worldwatch Pages 107* (March 1992), pp. 10–11.

World Resources Institute, *World Resources 1992–93: A Guide to Global Environment* (New York: Oxford University Press, 1992).

Edith Brown Weiss, Paul C. Szasz, and Daniel B. Magraw, *International Environmental Law: Basic Instruments and References* (Transnational Publishers Inc., 1991).

U.S. State Department, *A List of Treaties and Other International Agreements of the United States in Force on January 1, 1992* (U.S. Government Printing Office, March 1992).

United Nations Publication, *Multilateral Treaties Deposited with the Secretary General,* status as of December 31, 1991.

UNCED, *The Effectiveness of International Environmental Agreements* (ed. Peter H. Sand) (Cambridge, England: Grotius Publications Limited, 1992).

# Declaration of the Right to Nature Conservation, Environmental Protection and Sustainable Development

## I. General Principles, Rights and Responsibilities

### Fundamental Human Rights

1. All human beings have the fundamental right to an environment adequate for their health and well-being.

### Inter-Generational Equity

2. States shall conserve and use the environment and natural resources for the benefit of present and future generations.

### Conservation and Sustainable Use

3. States shall maintain ecosystems and ecological processes essential for the functioning of the biosphere, shall preserve biological diversity, and shall observe the principle of optimum sustainable yield in the use of living resources and ecosystems.

*Note:* This summary is based on the more detailed legal formulation in the report to the Brundtland Commission by the international legal experts group. It highlights only the main thrust of the principles and articles. This summary, presented by Thijs de la Court in *Beyond Brundtland* (New York: New Horizons Press, 1991), was included in the Brundtland Report as a draft and therefore was not an official proposal of the World Commission of Environment and Development.

## Environmental Standards and Monitoring

4. States shall establish adequate environmental protection standards and monitor changes in and publish relevant data on environmental quality and resource use.

## Prior Environmental Assessments

5. States shall make or require prior environmental assessments of proposed activities which may significantly affect the environment or use of a natural resource.

## Prior Notification, Access, and Due Process

6. States shall inform in a timely manner all persons likely to be significantly affected by a planned activity and grant them equal access and due process in administrative and judicial proceedings.

## Sustainable Development and Assistance

7. States shall ensure that conservation is treated as an integral part of the planning and implementation of development activities and provide assistance to other States, especially to developing countries, in support of environmental protection and sustainable development.

## General Obligation to Co-operate

8. States shall co-operate in good faith with other States in implementing the preceding rights and obligations.

# II. Principles, Rights and Obligations concerning Transboundary Natural Resources and Environmental Interferences

## Reasonable and Equitable Use

9. States shall use transboundary natural resources in a reasonable and equitable manner.

## Prevention and Abatement

10. States shall prevent or abate any transboundary environmental interference which could cause or causes significant harm (but subject to certain exceptions provided for in Art. 11 and Art. 12 below).

## Strict Liability

11. States shall take all reasonable precautionary measures to limit the risk when carrying out or permitting certain dangerous but beneficial activities and shall ensure that compensation is provided should substantial transboundary harm occur even when the activities were not known to be harmful at the time they were undertaken.

## Prior Agreements When Prevention Costs Greatly Exceed Harm

12. States shall enter into negotiations with the affected State on the equitable conditions under which the activity could be carried out when planning to carry out or permit activities causing transboundary harm which is substantial but far less than the cost of prevention. (If no agreement can be reached, see Art. 22.)

## Non-Discrimination

13. States shall apply as a minimum at least the same standards for environmental conduct and impacts regarding transboundary natural resources and environmental interferences as are applied domestically (i.e., do not do to others what you would not do to your own citizens).

## General Obligation to Co-operate on Transboundary Environmental Problems

14. States shall co-operate in good faith with other States to achieve optimal use of transboundary natural resources and effective prevention or abatement of transboundary interferences.

## Exchange of Information

15. States of origin shall provide timely and relevant information to the other concerned States regarding transboundary natural resources or environmental interferences.

## Prior Assessment and Notification

16. States shall provide prior and timely notification and relevant information to the other concerned States and shall make or require an environmental assessment of planned activities which may have significant transboundary effects.

## Prior Consultations

17. States of origin shall consult at an early stage and in good faith with other concerned States regarding existing or potential transboundary interferences with their use of a natural resources or the environment.

## Co-operative Arrangements for Environmental Assessment and Protection

18. States shall co-operate with the concerned States in monitoring, scientific research and standard setting regarding transboundary natural resources and environmental interferences.

## Emergency Situations

19. States shall develop contingency plans regarding emergency situations likely to cause transboundary environmental interferences and shall promptly warn, provide relevant information to and co-operate with concerned Stares about emergencies.

## Equal Access and Treatment

20. States shall grant equal access, due process and equal treatment in administrative and judicial proceedings to all persons who are or may be affected by transboundary interferences with their use of a natural resource or the environment.

# III. State Responsibility

21. States shall cease activities which breach an international obligation regarding the environment and provide compensation for the harm caused.

# IV. Peaceful Settlement of Disputes

22. States shall settle environmental disputes by peaceful means. If mutual agreement on a solution or on other dispute settlement arrangements is not reached within 18 months, the dispute shall be submitted to conciliation and, if unresolved, thereafter to arbitration or judicial settlement at the request of any of the concerned States.

# Notes

## Chapter 2. The Weaknesses of the Existing Environmental Treaty-Making System

1. De la Court is quoting Vandana Shiva and Jayanta Bandyopadhyay in *The Ecologist* 19, no. 3, (1989).

2. The magazine *Third World Resurgence* is replete, issue after issue, with literate and often well-documented attacks on the World Bank's investment practices.

3. De la Court cites Wouter Veening, of the international nature conservation organization IUCN, in the Dutch magazine *Natuur en Milieu*, April 1987, in describing the "fatal five" projects.

4. The UN Economic Commission for Africa and the Organization for Economic Cooperation and Development reported in 1987 on the economic dependence of Africa. The report is cited by de la Court.

5. Hilary F. French, "After the Earth Summit: The Future of Environmental Governance," Worldwatch Paper 107 (Washington, D.C.: Worldwatch Institute, March, 1992).

6. Of course, those who hold this view have a difficult time explaining why national governments have, from time to time, created multilateral institutions like the United Nations that have the power to force countries to change their behavior.

7. The United States, incidentally, is not a party to the Vienna Convention on the Law of Treaties, although it is considered binding by all U.S. courts. Eric Reifschneider, a student at Harvard Law School, helped me research the details of the Vienna Convention on Treaties. See Eric Reifschneider, " Creation of International Environmental Agreements," *Harvard Law Review* 104, no. 7 (1991).

8. Patricia Birnie, "The Role of International Law in Solving Certain Environmental Conflicts," in *International Environmental Diplomacy: The Management and Resolution of Transfrontier Environmental Problems,* ed. John Carroll (New York: Cambridge University Press, 1988).

9. The Mediterranean Action Plan is not listed in Appendix A. It is a regional, not a global, accord, although it is part of the Regional Seas Program managed by UNEP. See Peter Haas, *Saving the Mediterranean: The Politics of International Environmental Cooperation*, (New York, Columbia University Press, 1990).

10. See Roger Fisher, William Ury, with Bruce Patten, *Getting to Yes*, (Boston: Houghton Mifflin, Second edition, 1991); Roger Fisher and Scott Brown, *Getting Together*, (Boston: Houghton Mifflin, 1988); and Lawrence Susskind and Jeffrey Cruikshank, *Breaking the Impasse: Consensual Approaches to Resolving Public Disputes* (New York: Basic Books, 1987).

11. Caroline Thomas, *The Environment in International Relations* (London: Royal Institute of International Affairs, 1992).

12. Numerous instances of non-compliance (particularly with reporting requirements) are persented in Peter H. Sand, ed., *The Effectiveness of International Environmental Agreements*, Cambidge, Grotius Publications, 1992.

13. U.S. Citizens Network on the United Nations Conference on Environment and Development, *An Introductory Guide to the Earth Summit*, prepared by Mark Valentine. (San Francisco, 1991), pp. 12–13.

14. I have relied heavily on the Earth Summit Updates published monthly through 1992 by the Environmental and Energy Study Institute, 122 C Street, NW, Washington, D.C; and E and D File 1992, Briefings for NGOs on UNCED, published by the UN Nongovernmental Liaison Service, Geneva, Switzerland.

## Chapter 3. Representation and Voting

1. There is substantial disagreement about why the United States refused to sign the Biodiversity Convention. The head of the U.S. delegation to the Earth Summit, EPA Administrator William Reilly, was apparently trying up until the last possible moment to work out compromise language that would have allowed the United States to sign. However, he was undercut by the White House staff. Public statements from the Bush Administration suggest that the Biodiversity Convention was unacceptable because it required U.S. firms to pay continuing royalties and to share new patents and technological secrets with nations whose biological resources are the source of new products. Some observers point out that signing the Biodiversity Convention would have made it much more difficult for the administration to hold to its position that jobs should outweigh ecological considerations in the debate over protecting old-growth forests in the northwestern part of the United States. In the context of a presidential election, it seems that the White House took a position aimed at satisfying its business-oriented constituency.

2. Richard Benedick, "International Environmental Diplomacy" (Paper presented at the John F. Kennedy School of Government at Harvard University during the fall of 1991).

3. C. Berlet and W. Burke, "Corporate Fronts: Inside Anti-Environmentalism," *Greenpeace Magazine*, January-February-March, 1992.

4. Salah El Serafy, according to Daly, shows how to divide net receipts from a nonrenewable resource into an income component that can be consumed each year and a spatial component that must be invested each year in a renewable asset that yields a rate of return such that, at the end of the lifetime of the nonrenewable resource, a new renewable asset will have been built up to the point at which it can yield a perpetual stream equal to the income component of the depleted nonrenew-

able resource. See Salah El Serafy, "The Proper Calculation of Income from Depletable Natural Resources" in *Environmental Accounting for Sustainable Development: A UNDP-World Bank Symposium*, ed. Y. J. Ahmad, Salah El Serafy, and E. Lutz (Washington, D.C.: World Bank, 1989).

## Chapter 4. The Need for a Better Balance Between Science and Politics

1. Porter and Brown discuss the formation of veto coalitions in a number of places in their book, particularly on pages 23–24. They cite Fen Osler Hampson, "Climate Change: Building International Coalitions of the Like-minded," *International Journal* 45 (Winter 1989–1990): 36–74.

2. There is no official comprehensive listing and analysis of global environmental treaties published annually, but the following works are helpful: Fridtjof Nansen Institute, (Norway), *Green Globe Yearbook, 1992* New York: Oxford University Press, New York, 1992); and Alexandre Charles Kiss, ed., *Selected Multilateral Treaties in the Field of the Environment*, vols. 1 and 2 (Nairobi: United Nations Environment Programme, 1983) and UNCED's *The Effectiveness of International Environmental Agreements* (Peter Sands, ed.). I also found World Resources Institute, *World Resources 1992–93* (New York: Oxford University Press 1992), especially the final table, of great use.

3. The brief transboundary air pollution case study in Porter and Brown, pp. 71–74, is quite adamant about this point.

4. David Laws cites Beebee's report in Polar Research Board, *Antarctic Treaty System: An Assessment* (Washington, D.C.: National Academy Press, 1986).

5. Hilz and Radka cite a report about this UNEP study by R. F. Du Vivier, "Les Vaissaux du Poison: La Route des Dechets Toxiques," prepared in 1988.

6. Ruckelshaus's views appeared first in *Science* 221 (1983): 1026–28. He revised his views later in *Issues in Science and Technology*, Spring 1985, pp. 19–38.

7. I am grateful to Lasse Ringius for sharing early drafts of his dissertation on the London Dumping Convention, submitted to the European University Institute (Florence, Italy) in August 1992.

8. These discoveries and their importance to the negotiations process are presented by Thomas, *The Environment in International Relations*, pp. 199–237.

9. I. William Zartman, "International Environmental Negotiation: Challenges for Analysis and Practice," *Negotiation Journal* 8 (April 1992): 112–23.

10. For an excellent discussion of just how neutral can do this, see Connie Ozawa, *Recasting Science*, Boulder, Colo.: Westview Press, 1991.

11. For more on the emerging discipline of ecological economics, see the *Journal of Ecological Economics* published by the International Society for Ecological Economics (Amsterdam, Elsevier); and Robert Costanza, ed., *Ecological Economics: The Science and Management of Sustainability* (New York: Columbia University Press: 1991).

12. For a more complete discussion of sustainable development, see the special issue of *Environmental Impact Assessment Review*, May 1992, edited at the Massachusetts Institute of Technology and published by Elsevier Publishers. The

whole issue was devoted to an exploration of how the concept of sustainable development might be made more operational.

## Chapter 5. The Advantages and Disadvantages of Issue Linkage

1. The more recent debt-for-nature swaps involve transactions between sovereign states. Governments, as opposed to private organizations play the central roles. See Michael S. Sher, "Can Lawyers Save the Rainforest? Enforcing the Second Generation Debt-for-Nature Swaps," *Harvard Environmental Review* 17 (1993) for more details on the Polish Swap and others.

2. The terminology is that of Frances Cairncross, a journalist who writes for the *Economist*. See "Costing the Earth: Survey on the Environment," *Economist*, 2 September 1989, and her subsequent book by the same title.

3. See especially James Sebenius, "Negotiation Arithmetic: Adding and Subtracting Issues and Parties," *International Organization* 37 (Spring 1983).

4. Henry Kissinger, *White House Years* (Boston: Little, Brown, 1979), p. 129. This quotation is cited in Michael McGinnis, "Issue Linkage and the Evolution of Cooperation," *Journal of Conflict Resolution*, (March 1986): 141–70.

5. The GEF structure is still under discussion as it moves from a multiyear experiment to a more permanent status. At the Earth Summit, according to a Cable News Network interview with the GEF executive director broadcast from Brazil, the nations of the South were promised "a greater voice" in deciding GEF allocations. Subsequent conversations with GEF-affiliated staff suggest that individual projects will still undergo detailed review by GEF "scientific committees," and actual allocations will be voted on by both an advisory board (made up of recipient countries) and the three agencies (World Bank, UNDP, and UNEP) involved. For a more complete analysis of the difficulties lending institutions have reconciling their environmental policies and their economic development objectives, see Raymond F. Mikesell and Lawrence F. Williams, *International Banks and the Environment: From Growth to Sustainability—An Unfinished Agenda* (San Francisco: Sierra Club Books, 1992).

6. Steven Shrybman, "International Trade and the Environment (An Assessment of Present GATT Negotiations)" (Paper prepared for the Canadian Environmental Law Association, Toronto, October 1989).

7. *Commission of the European Communities v. Kingdom of Denmark*, Case 302/86, *Report of the Cases Before the Court*, vol. 8 (Luxembourg: Office for Official Publications of the European Communities, 1988).

8. For a more complete discussion of the possibilities of amending GATT see James O. Cameron, Thobeka Mjolo-Thamage, and Jonathan Robinson, "Relationship Between Environmental Agreements and Instruments Related to Trade and Development," in ed. Peter Sand, *The Effectiveness of International Environmental Agreements*, (1992), pp. 475–501.

## Chapter 6. Monitoring and Enforcement in the Face of Sovereignty

1. The report of the First Meeting of the Ad Hoc Working Group of Legal Experts on Non-compliance with the Montreal Protocol was presented in *Environ-

*mental Policy and Law* 19 (September 1989): 147–48. Note that a cursory review of more than one hundred environmental agreements revealed only three that had formal stipulations of international enforcement—and those did not deal with interference on sovereign territory—the rest dealt primarily with requirements regarding national legislation and judicial action, if anything at all. About one-third set up dispute-settlement procedures, and more than half required a formal routine data exchange. See *International Agreements to Protect the Environment and Wildlife* (Washington, D.C.: U.S. International Trade Commission, 1991).

2. This statement is attributed in the report of the meeting to Patrick Szell (United Kingdom), chairman of the meeting.

3. Stedman attributes this statement to A. Underdal, *The Politics of International Fisheries Management: The Case of the Northeast Atlantic* (Universiteforlaget, Oslo), who is cited in Steinar Andresen, "Science and Politics in the International Management of Whales," *Marine Policy*, 13, no 2 (1989): 99–117.

4. J. H. Ausubel and D. G. Victor, "Verification of International Environmental Agreement," *Annual Review of Energy and Environment, 1992*, vol. 17, p. 11, are less pessimistic about compliance with the Whaling Treaty than Stedman is. A General Accounting Office (U.S. Congress) Report published in January 1992 concluded that "international environmental agreements are not well monitored." International Environment: International Agreements Are Not Well Monitored," GAO/RCED-92-43.

5. The "revolutionary nature" of the Hague Declaration is underscored by Hillary F. French, "After the Earth Summit: The Future of Environmental Governance," Worldwatch Paper 107, (Washington, D.C.: Worldwatch Institute, 1992), p. 35.

6. The 1989 draft of a code of ecological security was presented at the early drafting sessions by the Soviets participating in the drafting of the Salzburg Initiative.

7. Antonia and Abram Chayes are completing a book on compliance. Their ideas on compliance were presented initially in Abram Chayes and Antonia H. Chayes, "Adjustment and Compliance Processes in International Regulatory Regimes," in *Preserving the Global Environment: The Challenge of Shared Leadership*, ed. Jessica Tuchman Mathews (New York: Norton, 1991), and Abram Chayes and Antonia H. Chayes, "Compliance Without Enforcement: State Behavior Under Regulatory Treaties," *Negotiation Journal* 7 July 1991. Their book will present more about the merits of various kinds of sanctions and ways of achieving greater transparency. Abram and Antonia Chayes, along with William Pace, head of the Eco-Start Project at the Center for Development of International Law in Washington, D.C., have been exploring the ways in which environmental treaty verification and enforcement might build on the experience in the arms control field.

8. Thomas Schelling, *Strategy of Conflict* (Cambridge: Harvard University Press, 1960).

9. For a helpful overview of the environmental dispute resolution provisions contained in global and regional environmental treaties see Profullachandra N. Bhagwati, "Environmental Disputes," in ed. Peter Sand, *The Effectiveness of International Environmental Agreements* (1992), pp. 436–452.

10. Oran Young, "The Effectiveness of International Institution: Hard Cases and Critical Variables," in *Governance Without Government: Order and Change in World Politics*, ed. James N. Rosenau and Ernst-Otto Czempiel pp. 160–92 (Cambridge: Cambridge University Press, 1992).

11. I am grateful to Susan O'Rourke for sharing her paper, "Using the Amnesty International Organization as a Model for Green Amnesty International, an Environmental International Grass-Roots Organization Using the Existing United Nations Human Rights Framework to Promote International Environmental Protection" (Submitted to the Seminar on International Environmental Negotiation at the Program on Negotiation at Harvard Law School, December 1991).

12. These ideas were worked out in conjunction with my colleagues Lawrence Bacow and Michael Wheeler. See their book *Environmental Dispute Resolution* (New York: Plenum, 1984) for more details.

13. The only summary of non-compliance data on a treaty-by-treaty basis is presented (in a very sketchy form) in Peter H. Sands, ed., *The Effectiveness of International Environmental Agreements* (1992).

## Chapter 7. Reforming the System

1. An additional result of these sessions was the creation of the International Environmental Negotiation Network (IENN). The network is an informal association committed to advancing the reforms presented in the Salzburg Initiative and promoting long-term capacity building for more effective environmental treaty making. The IENN has been working to recruit at least ten representatives (two senior government officials, two grass-roots environmental activists, two business leaders, two scientists, and two journalists) from a minimum of one hundred countries. IENN members have made presentations at most of the global environmental meetings that have been held since 1990, including the Earth Summit. In addition, IENN publishes a newspaper (*concordare*) three times a year that highlights examples of successful efforts to build long-term capacity for global environmental management, emphasizing strategies such as (computer-based) methods of information sharing and technology transfer; preparation of advanced training materials and teaching tools; programs for enhancing public awareness of and participation in environmental decision making; creation of new North-South alliances; and the building of organizational networks to facilitate global cooperation.

2. See Lawrence Susskind, Eileen Babbit, and Phyllis Segal, "The Federal ADR Act: Progress and Prospects," *Negotiation Journal*, 9(1) (January 1993): 59–75, for a description of the Negotiated Rulemaking Act and an analysis of the formation and use of rosters for selecting mediators.

3. For a detailed analysis of the U.S. experience, see Alfred Marcus, "Environmental Protection Agency," in *The Politics of Regulation*, ed. James Q. Wilson, pp. 267–303 (New York: Basic Books, 1980).

4. I am indebted to Dr. Bert Metz, a member of the Dutch negotiating team at the Earth Summit, for sharing his version of a "three-layered package" for the

Climate Change Convention. My conversations with Metz and Marius Einthoven, director-general for the environment in the Dutch government, helped to clarify the importance of synchronized expectations.

5. Peter M. Haas, Robert O. Keohane, Mark A. Levy eds., *Institutions for the Earth: Sources of Effective International Environmental Protection* (Cambridge: MIT Press, forthcoming).

# Selected Readings

## General Background

Four books provide an excellent introduction to the fundamentals of global environmental decision making. Lynton Caldwell's *International Environmental Policy: Emergence and Dimensions*, 2d ed. (Durham: Duke University Press, 1990) introduces the basic multilateral institutional arrangements through which global environmental policies are made. It also provides an excellent summary of the 1972 Stockholm Conference, which, in various ways, marked the beginning of the current "era" of global environmental diplomacy. Oran Young's *International Cooperation: Building Regimes for Natural Resources and the Environment* (Ithaca: Cornell University Press, 1989) explains the dynamics of international bargaining as it relates to environmental resource management. Jessica Tuchman Mathews, *Preserving the Global Environment: The Challenge of Shared Leadership* (New York: Norton, 1991), offers an edited collection of essays pinpointing the trade-offs that must sometimes be made between environmental protection and economic and social development. This collection also demonstrates that environmental issues are now very high on the international political agenda. Finally, another collection, *International Environmental Diplomacy: The Management and Resolution of Transfrontier Environmental Problems*, ed. John Carroll (New York: University of Cambridge Press, 1988), summarizes the underlying legal and political obstacles to global environmental cooperation.

The World Resources Institute, in collaboration with the UN Environment Programme and the UN Development Programme, offers *World Resources, 1992–93: A Guide to the Global Environment* (New York: Oxford University Press, 1992). This volume provides an overview of the key environmental trends that trigger and constrain global diplomacy.

## Case Studies

Several sets of case studies provided the basis for much of the analysis presented in this book. These have been published in two volumes: Lawrence Susskind, Esther Siskind, and J. William Breslin, *Nine Case Studies in International Environmental*

*Negotiation* (Cambridge: MIT-Harvard Public Disputes Program, 1990) and Lawrence Susskind, Eric Dolin, and J. William Breslin, *International Environmental Treaty-Making* (Cambridge: Program on Negotiation at Harvard Law School, 1992). The first volume includes the following cases studies: "Debt-for-Nature Swaps" by Kristin Dawkins; "The Montreal Protocol on Substances That Deplete the Ozone Layer" by Chris Granda; "Negotiations over Auto Emissions Standards in the European Community 1983–1989" by Mark Corrales and Tony Dreyfus; "The Basel Convention on Transboundary Movement of Hazardous Wastes and Their Disposal" by Christopher Hilz and Mark Radka; "Ivory, Elephants, or Both: Negotiating the Transfer of the African Elephant to an Appendix II Within CITES" by Thomas E. Arend, Jr.; "The Antarctic Minerals Regime Negotiations" by David Laws; "The International Whaling Commission and Negotiation for a Global Moratorium on Whaling" by Bruce J. Stedman; "Progress Toward Canadian-U.S. Acid Rain Control" by William L. Schroeer; and "The Convention on Early Notification and on Assistance in the Case of Nuclear Attack" by Sorin Bodea. The second volume includes "Nongovernmental Organizations: Their Past, Present, and Future Role in International Environmental Negotiations" by Nancy Lindborg; "Secretariats and International Environmental Negotiations: Two New Models" by Rosemary Sandford; "Using Computer Networks to Improve Prenegotiation Discussions and Alliances for Global Environmental Action" by John W. Wilson; "The Remote Sensing Regime: Sources of Instability, Options for Reform, and Implications for Environmental Treatymaking" by Ian Simm; "Tropical Deforestation and International Environmental Negotiation: An Illustration of the North-South Confrontation" by Marcella Obdrzalek; "The International Joint Commission: A Possible Model for International Resource Management" by Carol Reardon; "The Convention on Biological Diversity: Negotiating a Global Regime" by Martha Rojas and Chris Thomas; "Strengthening UNEP to Improve Environmental Treaty Compliance" by Joseph Mbuna; and "Improving Compliance Provisions in International Environmental Agreements" by David Mulenex.

UNCED published *The Effectiveness of International Environmental Agreements* (ed. Peter H. Sand), Cambridge, England: Grotius Publications Limited, 1992) with summaries of 124 treaties.

## The Earth Summit

There are many reviews and interpretations of what happened at the UN-sponsored Earth Summit in Brazil in June 1992. An early report, including highlights of the documents produced, was prepared by Peter Haas, Edward Parsons, and Marc Levy and appeared in *Environment* (published by Heldref Publications in Washington, D.C., in cooperation with the Scientists' Institute for Public Information) 34 (October 1992). For a detailed review of all the preconference meetings leading up to the Earth Summit, see the journal *Environmental Policy and Law*, published every other month by the International Council on Environmental Law (ICEL), Adenaurallee 214, D-5300 Bonn, Germany.

## The Weaknesses of the Environmental Treaty-Making System

The starting point for much of the debate about the strengths and weaknesses of the existing environmental-treaty-making system is the report of the World Commission on Environment and Development, *Our Common Future* (Oxford: Oxford University Press, 1987). This UN sponsored study popularized the term *sustainable development* and offered a set of detailed case studies that underscore the link between environmental protection and economic growth. Thijs de la Court, *Beyond Brundtland: Green Development in the 1990s* (New York: New Horizons Books, 1990), summarizes the reaction of the developing world to the World Commission report.

To appreciate fully the criticisms of the existing convention-protocol approach to environmental treaty making, it is necessary to review the basics of negotiation theory. Roger Fisher, William Ury, and Bruce Patton, in *Getting to YES: Negotiating Agreement Without Giving In*, 2d ed. (New York: Penguin Books, 1991), provide a general framework for thinking about what works and what doesn't work in negotiation. Fisher's earlier book, *International Conflict for Beginners* (New York: Harper and Row, 1969), offers a brief introduction to the dynamics of international bargaining. Lawrence Susskind and Jeffrey Cruikshank, *Breaking the Impasse: Consensual Approaches to Resolving Public Disputes* (New York: Basic Books, 1987), reviews the key assumptions about multiparty, multi-issue negotiation and the steps involved in consensus building on complex public policy matters. Howard Raiffa, in *The Art and Science of Negotiation* (Cambridge: Harvard University Press, 1982), offers a more complete and formal analysis of negotiation theory.

Caroline Thomas, *The Environment in International Relations* (London: Royal Institute of International Affairs, 1992), nicely highlights some of the conflicts between the developed and developing nations on environmental issues. Arthur A. Stein, *Why Nations Cooperate: Circumstances and Choice in International Relations* (Ithaca: Cornell University Press, 1990), summarizes the thinking of political science and international relations theorists on the meaning and importance of national sovereignty. And Gareth Porter and Jane Welsch Brown, *Global Environmental Politics* (Boulder, Colo.: Westview Press, 1991), offers an in-depth review of the politics of both North-South relations and sovereignty, but the perspective and role of the international business community are best presented in Stephen Schmidheiny, *Changing Course: A Global Business Perspective on Development and the Environment*, (Cambridge: MIT Press, 1992). The question of who might represent the interests of future generations in international negotiations is beautifully presented by Edith Weiss Brown, *In Fairness to Future Generations: International Law, Common Patrimony and Intergenerational Equity* (Tokyo: United Nations University and Dobbs Ferry; New York: Transnational Publishers, 1989).

Sustainability is described and discussed in a number of books. The five that I find most helpful are Herman Daly, *Steady State Economics*, 2d ed. (Washington, D.C.: Island Press, 1991); David Pearce, Edward Barbier, and Anil Markandya,

*Sustainable Development: Economics and Environment in the Third World*, (London: Earthscan, 1990); Lester Milbrath, *Envisioning a Sustainable Society: Learning Our Way Out* (Albany: State University of New York Press, 1989); Robert Costanza, ed., *Ecological Economics: The Science and Management of Sustainability* (New York: Columbia University Press, 1991); and Herman Daly and John B. Cobb, *For the Common Good*, (Boston: Beacon Press, 1989).

## The Need for a Balance Between Science and Politics

The single best discussions of the basic scientific considerations in global environmental treaty making can be found in Cheryl Silver, *One Earth, One Future: Our Changing Global Environment* (Washington, D.C.: National Academy Press, 1990), and Daniel Botkin, *Discordant Harmonies: A New Ecology for the Twenty-first Century* (New York: Oxford University Press, 1990). To understand more about the mechanics of ecological catastrophe, see Derek Ellis, *Environments at Risk: Case Histories of Impact Assessment* (Berlin: Springer-Verlag, 1989). For more on the negotiation of the Montreal Protocol, see Richard Elliott Benedick, *Ozone Diplomacy: New Directions in Safeguarding the Planet* (Cambridge: Harvard University Press, 1991). One of the best overviews of risk perception and risk management is in Jennifer Brown, ed., *Environmental Threats: Perception, Analysis, and Management* (London: Belhaven Press, 1989).

Peter Haas presents the idea of "epistemic communities" in "Do Regimes Matter? Epistemic Communities and Mediterranean Pollution Control," *International Organization* 43 (Summer 1989); 378–403, and more completely in *Saving the Mediterranean: The Politics of International Environmental Cooperation*, (New York: Columbia University Press, 1990). In thinking further about the role of scientists in global environmental decision making, I was also impressed with Lynton Caldwell, *Between Two Worlds: Science, the Environmental Movement and Policy Choice* (New York: Cambridge University Press, 1990).

Michael Jacobs, *The Green Economy: Environment, Sustainable Development and the Politics of the Future* (London: Pluto Press, 1991), and Mark Sagoff, *The Economy of the Earth: Philosophy, Law and the Environment* (New York: Cambridge University Press, 1988), present effective critiques of cost-benefit analysis leading to my preference for ecological economics over classical environmental economics.

## Issue Linkage

The pioneer in this field is James Sebenius, whose *Negotiating the Law of the Sea* (Cambridge: Harvard University Press, 1984) introduced the idea of "negotiation arithmetic"—strategic addition and subtraction of parties and issues to achieve specific negotiated results. He built on the work of Howard Raiffa, *The Art and Science of Negotiation* (Cambridge: Harvard University Press, 1982). I also found I. William Zartman and Maureen Berman, *The Practical Negotiator* (New Haven: Yale University Press, 1982) instructive. The link between international and domestic negotiations is presented succinctly in Robert Putnam, "Diplomacy and

Domestic Politics: The Logic of Two-level Games," *International Organization* 42 (1982): 427–460. Crucial insight is also provided by Jessica Tuchman Mathews, "Redefining Security," *Foreign Affairs* 68 (Spring 1989): 162–77. She was the first to underscore the absolute necessity of linking environmental issues with economic and security negotiations.

Linkage must be viewed in terms of the impact it has on the relationships among countries. These are well analyzed in Roger Fisher and Scott Brown, *Getting Together* (Boston: Houghton Mifflin, 1989). The use of threats in negotiation is best summarized in Thomas Schelling, *The Strategy of Conflict* (Cambridge: Harvard University Press, 1960).

## Monitoring and Enforcement

Abram and Antonia Chayes write about compliance with international treaties. Their basic thesis, (that most countries are likely to comply with most global environmental treaties most of the time, even if there is not a strong threat that penalties will be imposed upon noncompliers), is presented in "Compliance Without Enforcement: State Behavior Under Regulatory Treaties," *Negotiation Journal* 7 (1991): 311. For more about the reasons that people (and by extension, governments) do and don't comply with regulations, see Jane Mansbridge, ed., *Beyond Self-Interest*, (Chicago: University of Chicago Press, 1992). Roger Fisher explains why and how compliance with laws might be enhanced in *Improving Compliance with International Law* (Charlottesville: University of Virginia Press, 1981). Robert Axelrod explains why, in sustained relationships, parties decide it is in their self-interest to live up to their promises and obligations in *The Evolution of Cooperation* (New York: Basic Books, 1984). Finally, Elinor Ostrom, *Managing the Commons* (New York: Cambridge University Press, 1991), demonstrates that parties sharing a common resource are not doomed to overexploiting that resource, even if there is not a strong central authority to control short-term selfish impulses to maximize at the expense of others.

# Index